T0048831

The Art of SERIES

EDITED BY CHARLES BAXTER

The Art of series is a line of books reinvigorating the practice of craft and criticism. Each book is a brief, witty, and useful exploration of fiction, nonfiction, or poetry by a writer impassioned by a singular craft issue. *The Art of* volumes provide a series of sustained examinations of key, but sometimes neglected, aspects of creative writing by some of contemporary literature's finest practitioners.

The Art of Intimacy: The Space Between
    by Stacey D'Erasmo

The Art of Description: World into Word by Mark Doty

The Art of the Poetic Line by James Longenbach

The Art of Daring: Risk, Restlessness, Imagination
    by Carl Phillips

The Art of Attention: A Poet's Eye by Donald Revell

The Art of Time in Fiction: As Long As It Takes
    by Joan Silber

The Art of Syntax: Rhythm of Thought, Rhythm of Song
    by Ellen Bryant Voigt

*The Art of Recklessness: Poetry as Assertive Force and
    Contradiction* by Dean Young

THE ART OF

TIME IN FICTION

AS LONG AS IT TAKES

Other Books by Joan Silber

The Size of the World
Ideas of Heaven
Lucky Us
In My Other Life
In the City
Household Words

The Art of

TIME IN FICTION

AS LONG AS IT TAKES

Joan Silber

Graywolf Press

Publication of this volume is made possible in part by a grant provided by
the Minnesota State Arts Board, through an appropriation by the Minnesota
State Legislature; a grant from the Wells Fargo Foundation Minnesota; and
a grant from the National Endowment for the Arts, which believes that a
great nation deserves great art. Significant support has also been provided
by the Bush Foundation; Target; the McKnight Foundation; and other gener-
ous contributions from foundations, corporations, and individuals. To these
organizations and individuals we offer our heartfelt thanks.

NATIONAL
ENDOWMENT
FOR THE ARTS

MINNESOTA
STATE ARTS BOARD

WELLS
FARGO

TARGET.

Published by Graywolf Press
250 Third Avenue North, Suite 600
Minneapolis, Minnesota 55401
All rights reserved.

www.graywolfpress.org

Published in the United States of America

ISBN 978-1-55597-530-2

8 10 12 14 16 15 13 11 9

Library of Congress Control Number: 2008941980

Series cover design: Scott Sorenson

Cover art: Scott Sorenson

It is quite true what Philosophy says: that Life must be understood backwards. But that makes one forget the other saying: that it must be lived—forwards. The more one ponders this, the more it comes to mean that life in the temporal existence never becomes quite intelligible, precisely because at no moment can I find complete quiet to take the backward-looking position.

—*The Diary of Søren Kierkegaard*

Contents

THE ART OF

TIME IN FICTION

AS LONG AS IT TAKES

Introduction

Time draws the shapes of stories. Here's a story everyone knows: A young girl—gentle, somewhat naive—works in a kindergarten instead of going off to university; she likes children and will probably marry before long anyway—she's pretty and comes from money. And indeed she's soon engaged, to a man who's a bit older but a great celebrity. He's a prince of England! His family's doctors determine she is a virgin, and his mother, not an easy woman, is pleased at his choice. The girl is shy—reporters make her cry—but she does her best. Which is very good—she is soon more popular than the queen. She becomes pregnant before her honeymoon is over and is really very happy to be a young mother. How beautifully she has risen to her role. People think of her as a rare person who is worthy of her good luck.

But wait, there's more. She discovers that her husband has been seeing an old girlfriend on the side. She grows bitter, develops eating disorders, takes lovers of her own. After much struggle, she and her husband divorce. She is still the princess of people's hearts. Reporters, excited by her story, chase her and her lover through a tunnel, and the car crashes and she is killed. Public love has killed her.

But wait. Her husband, who has never been happy, settles down at last with the woman whom he has loved all along. She is dowdy and no longer young, and she suits him very well. He once sent her bawdy messages on his cell phone, and they were a joke to people. Public love, he decides, is beside the point.

I offer these three paragraphs as simple examples of how a story is entirely determined by what portion of time it chooses to narrate. Where the teller begins and ends a tale decides what its point is, how it gathers meaning. Yogi Berra's famous bit of hope about a ball game—it ain't over till it's over—is the storyteller's dilemma. When *is* it over? And of all the choices a writer makes, a story's allotment of time can be the least conscious. This book is meant as a reminder of the range of what is possible, a reflection on richly various visions and methods.

My own fiction has made me brood on this topic with the necessary intensity of someone who's unwittingly chosen the hard way. I'm interested in how fates roll out over many years and am drawn to write fiction that takes on the task of compressing whole lifetimes into short stories or chapters. It's pretty easy to see how this might be done badly—thinly imagined, clumsily summarized—and sometimes difficult to see how it can be done at all.

The work of this has led me back to the elementary notion that all fiction has to contend with the experience of time passing. First one thing happens and then another: that's a story for you. This parade of events is what distinguishes the narrative impulse from the purely lyrical one. A poem can carry out its investigations within an endless moment, it can abide in stillness if it wants to, but fiction pretty much has to unfold in sequence. A story can arrange events in any order it finds useful, but it does have to move between then and now and later.

In his novel *The Red and the Black,* Stendhal prefaces one of the chapters with the epigram (attributed to Saint-Réal) "A novel is a mirror that is carried along a road." It's an awkward image –I've always imagined someone hauling a heavy pier glass over a nineteenth-century highway—and for years I thought it was just another way of saying art is a mirror held up to nature. Later I saw that it's the *road* that Stendhal is pointing to—the long and winding trail that keeps a writer on the move, toting that mirror over hill and dale—and the road is time.

Here's a tale in its most basic shape: In the fullness of summer, a happy grasshopper sings and dances all day, and when he sees an ant working to haul a grain of wheat to store for winter, he invites the ant to take a break and party instead, insisting there's plenty to eat right now, why worry? When the cold weather comes, the grasshopper has no food at all and he dies watching the ant eat its stored food. No mercy from the ant. It's a traditional plot—a crucial choice and its outcome. A decision is rewarded or punished. Aesop's moral here— *think ahead*—is illustrated by the progression of cause and effect. The high-stepping grasshopper, however well he sings, is swept along by the causality of story. And time is its agent, summer to winter.

The reckless grasshopper made his choice. E. M. Forster, in *Aspects of the Novel,* famously says that if we're told the king died and then the queen died, that's a story, but if someone says the king died and then the queen died of grief, that's a plot. Plot likes causation. We read anything looking for a pattern of events, and through it a meaning—the reason someone is bothering to tell us this. Plot is how a writer indicates the ways she or he thinks the world works.

So how much time does it take for an outcome to manifest itself? Some results happen instantly; some take decades to cook. I seemed to have grown up with the sense that most short stories—from Edgar Allan Poe's "The Tell-Tale Heart" to Katherine Mansfield's "Bliss"— were organized around a single scene or a brief, tight arrangement of scenes. But I knew there were counter-examples, stories that skipped across decades; Chekhov's "The Darling" took place over a good twenty years or so.

(I had discovered Chekhov as a teenager and he was one of the authors who made me want to be a writer.) I did naturally think that novels all had longer time spans than stories, until I encountered James Joyce's *Ulysses,* a novel that took place in a single day, all seven hundred and eighty-three pages of it. Tradition, resistance to tradition, private experience, and innate belief go into any author's choice of how many imagined minutes or years a story needs to make itself clear and felt. How much time it covers has everything to do with what it means.

In our daily lives, anyone reporting an episode knows this. We can narrate what happened during, say, a lovers' quarrel by staying within the confines of the scene itself, or by harking back to earlier times, earlier causes and effects, other characters' histories. A bad storyteller will make us beg *just get to the point,* and a good storyteller will make us beg for more. Technique is needed, and the same skills will not serve for all approaches to time.

To talk, as any writer does, of capturing, framing, and leaping across time, is to lean on metaphors to report on the ephemeral. It's the fiction writer's task to put the reader through the strangely desirable misapprehension that three decades have passed during the five hours it took to read certain pages. Albert Einstein said, "Us physicists believe the separation between past, present, and future is only an illusion, although a convincing one." No mortal can really cut or slow or speed up time. Why do we think we've lived through all the years of David Copperfield's youth? This suggests—and I'll try to say more about this—that time is always in some way the subject of fiction.

Kierkegaard famously said—in a quote I've used as this book's epigraph—that life can only be understood backward but has to be lived forward. However, fiction (this is one of its consolations) imagines for us a stopping point from which life can be seen as intelligible—the "complete quiet" (another translation of Kierkegaard calls this the "necessary resting place") that allows for understanding, the angle of retrospect, which is the storyteller's premise. A story is already over before we hear it. That is how the teller knows what it means.

Because meaning is determined by where a story ends, I want to look at time in fiction by considering this question of duration, the span of time selected for a story's events. All the dilemmas in organizing time are grounded in this first decision about how long it takes. When I started looking at favorite works of fiction, I came up with a few basic categories for time spans, handy labels. This book will look at classic time (a brief natural span—a month, a season, a year—handled in scene-and-summary), long time (decades, lifetimes), switchback time (moving back and forth among points in past and present), slowed time (brief instants in detail), and fabulous time (a way to think about non-realistic fiction). These are meant as convenient sub-divisions of an endless reading list. I want to look closely at the techniques needed for each category and to think about what draws writers to their choices. My list pretends in no way to be the final cut in possibilities—there's no tent big enough to cover what fiction can do with time.

I'd like to come back at the end to consider the notion of time as content. Writing this has convinced me that any fiction writer, obliged to evoke the experience of time passing, is up against the human conundrum of time slipping away, what Buddhists call impermanence. I want to look more closely at stories whose plots directly address remembering, forgetting, and wasting time, as well as fiction featuring imaginative play about time's rules. A crucial last example will look at the contrast in how different cultures measure time. Some final remarks about containment, borders, finality, and death will bring the book to its close.

Classic Time

Most of us, as readers, can love a book with great devotion and know its every part in detail without bothering to think much about its time scheme. Only when a book does something out of the usual do we register a response. So I thought I would begin with exactly the fiction that attracts no notice in its treatment of time, that follows an approach readers take for granted. *Classic time* is the term I've come up with to describe the default mode in twentieth- and twenty-first-century fiction. A favorite assumption—in writing workshops, in books on writing, and in the ordinary conversations of lay readers—is that a story or a novel will rely chiefly on scene, carefully interspersed with a little necessary summary. Summary is by its nature weaker, aspiring writers are often told, but it helps avoid the too-slow literalness of scene after scene. In novels that might serve as examples of classic time, the span is short enough to be easily seen as a unity and is often delineated by a natural border—a month, a season, a year. F. Scott Fitzgerald's *The Great Gatsby* is a beautiful example of this classic pattern.

The duration of *The Great Gatsby*'s plot is a single summer. The sun glows, burns, and fades in its story line. East and West Egg, those imaginary spots "on that slender riotous island which extends itself due east of New York," are most attractive in the warm season, and summer weather features heavily in crucial scenes. When Nick first sees his cousin Daisy again, she and her friend Jordan have opened all the windows to let in the "warm windy afternoon" and their dresses are "rippling and fluttering" while the curtains "whip and snap." Nick is happily watching them when Daisy's husband, Tom Buchanan, shuts the rear windows and puts a stop to all the lovely ballooning motion. Summer rain drenches Gatsby in the scene when he is waiting outside Nick's door to see Daisy at last. Gatsby's huge parties take place on his vast lawns in the summer nights. The searing heat is what makes Daisy insist that the entire ill-assorted luncheon group—Daisy, Tom, Gatsby, Nick, Jordan—must drive into town to get away from the sun, and once they're in the city they rent a suite at the Plaza with the notion that it will be cooler there. Gatsby's funeral takes place just at the time when all the houses along Long Island Sound are closing for the end of the season.

Much happens in that summer. Though *Gatsby* is short—my Scribner's paperback is 121 pages—I've never heard anyone call it a novella, only a novel. This is probably because it's so packed with event; novellas tend to be narrowly focused. There is a surprising amount of high action in the story—three people are dead at the end, like bodies onstage in an Elizabethan tragedy—and the events rise with great force to the climax of Gatsby's death (a murder by mistake, whose causes include the vanity of Daisy's bad driving and the malevolence of Tom's false report to Myrtle's husband).

One of the mysteries of craft in the book is how a novel written largely in scene has a plot that happens to depend on the past. Gatsby, some five years before, was a young soldier about to go to war who won Daisy's heart and has never forgotten it. Much fiction depends on people who never forget. This clinging, this refusal to "get over it," is very useful in fiction, however inadvisable it may be in real life. Other examples of stories that rest on this same stubbornness are discussed in the final section of this book.

The engine behind *The Great Gatsby*'s story is Gatsby's colossal resolve to get Daisy back, despite all odds. Nick, a little alarmed at Gatsby's romantic certainty, suggests that he shouldn't ask too much of Daisy:

> "You can't repeat the past."
>
>   "Can't repeat the past?" he cried incredulously. "Why of course you can!"

If Nick is our narrator, and he has only just met Gatsby, what does he know of that past? One of my

favorite parts of the novel shows Fitzgerald's elegant solution to the dilemma of requiring backstory that the narrator himself has never witnessed. Lesser novelists resort
to eavesdropping, convenient confessions, or neighborhood hearsay, but Fitzgerald's device has more intimacy
and more poetry. During the book's first scene at one of
Gatsby's fabulously glamorous parties, Gatsby summons
Jordan, who's known Daisy since their Louisville girl-
hood, into a private room for a talk. "I've just heard the
most amazing thing," Jordan tells Nick. Fourteen pages
later, during lunch at the Plaza, she tells him a story. In
Louisville, she once saw the very popular Daisy with an
adoring young officer named Jay Gatsby, and later there
were rumors that Daisy was caught packing a suitcase to
say good-bye to a soldier in New York, but within a year
she was engaged to the much wealthier Tom. Half an
hour before the bridal dinner, Jordan, a bridesmaid, came
into the room and found Daisy, "drunk as a monkey," with
a letter in her hand. Jordan says she was frightened to
see a girl so drunk. Daisy, who'd thrown her bridal pearl
necklace into the wastebasket, kept saying,

> "Tell 'em all Daisy's change' her mind."
>   She began to cry—she cried and cried. I rushed
> out and found her mother's maid, and we locked the
> door and got her into a cold bath. She wouldn't let
> go of the letter. She took it into the tub with her and
> squeezed it up into a wet ball, and only let me leave it

in the soap-dish when she saw that it was coming to pieces like snow.

Fitzgerald has used Jordan (a secondary character) to render as scene what might easily have been cast as summary. It's worth noting how Fitzgerald avoids having Jordan closely narrate the affair itself, but instead invents a culminating episode—a drunken Daisy torn by regret and heartbreak, a condition we never see her in again. And indeed the rest of Jordan's account tells how Daisy married Tom the next night "without so much as a shiver" and returned from her honeymoon seemingly enthralled. We keep that glowing nugget of back-story (Daisy in the tub, weeping for Gatsby) through the unfolding of their latter-day affair—evidence that something real did once happen between them.

Fitzgerald's instinct is always for the immediacy of scene. One of the fullest, most striking scenes in the novel is the afternoon when Nick has consented to invite Daisy over for tea so that Gatsby can be reintroduced to her. The overwrought Gatsby almost leaves because he can't stand waiting. Daisy comes on scene bantering to Nick—"Is this absolutely where you live, my dearest one?" They enter the house, but no Gatsby is in sight. In a bit of stagecraft, he has decided to go out and come in again, to make a ridiculous, puddle-splashed entrance. Dumbstruck at seeing each other, both Daisy and Gatsby are entirely artificial at first, and Gatsby leans on the mantel with such fake nonchalance he almost knocks over a clock. When Gatsby runs to the kitchen to say what a "terrible, terrible mistake" this is, Nick scolds him back into the room and waits out in the rainy yard himself, pausing for a half hour while the ex-lovers make up. The choreography could not be more like a comic farce, with characters exiting and entering through the rooms of the set. And the lovers have altered dramatically when Gatsby goes back into the house—Daisy's face is tearstained and Gatsby is glowing.

Gatsby next wants to show Daisy his fabulous house, the mansion that is the totem of his new identity, acquired with Daisy in mind. In the bedroom, Daisy takes up a gold brush from Gatsby's dresser and smooths her hair, "whereupon Gatsby sat down and shaded his eyes and began to laugh":

> "It's the funniest thing, old sport," he said hilariously. "I can't—when I try to—"
>
> He had passed visibly through two states and was entering upon a third. After his embarrassment and his unreasoning joy he was consumed with wonder at her presence. He had been full of the idea so long, dreamed it right through to the end, waited with his teeth set, so to speak, at an inconceivable bit of intensity. Now, in the reaction, he was himself running down like an overwound clock.

The scene ends with Daisy in her own moment of wonder, contemplating the heap of luxurious shirts that Gatsby has thrown down from his shelves: "'They're such beautiful shirts,' she sobbed, her voice muffled in the thick folds. 'It makes me sad because I've never seen such—such beautiful shirts before.'"

The scene's power rests on dialogue and gesture. Gatsby and Daisy both have stylized ways of speaking. Daisy is committed to a rippling archness, and Gatsby has the strain of calculated masquerade in most of his sentences. This allows for considerable economy in presenting them—they are very vivid, and a little goes a long way. When they speak more frankly, they are in a state where talk has become utterance—they can't not say the phrases that break through. I point this out because immediacy in scenes is sometimes taken to mean a slavish step-by-step presentation of moments. The brilliance of Fitzgerald's scenes has to do with their concentration—they are distilled into flashes and are far from a blow-by-blow report in real time. Gesture aids this. Fitzgerald draws Gatsby as a man whose body is overtaken by his obsession: he can hardly stay still, he dashes away in terror, he flings around his shirts.

It's also a highly inflected scene (i.e., not flat), rising to the high point of Gatsby's triumph in rekindling love in Daisy (at least for a while). This is, of course, the essence of narrative time. Elements are reduced to their service to the story—time passes in order to reach the

point of crisis. The beauty of selective concreteness—
dialogue, gesture, sensory detail—is that it allows us to
believe we have experienced the time completely. "We
were there" for the good parts.

Skilled as Fitzgerald is at shirking from summary, he is
perfectly happy (sometimes too happy) to frame events
with commentaries; Nick's opening and closing mono-
logues are summings up, studded with epigrams. More
worthy as examples of time summarized are the ac-
counts of Gatsby's parties. The parties happen over and
over; they are numberless and endless. (Only the chronic
guest Klipspringer, nicknamed the boarder, has been to
them all.) How to give a generalized report, without blur-
ring and dulling the effect, while also conveying the mas-
sive repetition of a pattern? "From East Egg, then, came
the Chester Beckers and the Leeches, and a man named
Bunsen, whom I knew at Yale, and Doctor Webster Civet,
who was drowned last summer up in Maine." Fitzgerald's
guest list goes on for six paragraphs, studded with pithy
details:

> Snell was there three days before he went to the peni-
> tentiary, so drunk out on the gravel drive that Mrs.
> Ulysses Swett's automobile ran over his right hand. . . .
>   Benny McClenahan arrived always with four girls.
> They were never quite the same ones in physical

person, but they were so identical one with another that it inevitably seemed they had been there before . . . and their last names were either the melodious names of flowers and months or the sterner ones of the great American capitalists whose cousins, if pressed, they would confess themselves to be. . . .

And Miss Claudia Hip, with a man reputed to be her chauffeur, and a prince of something, whom we called Duke, and whose name, if I ever knew it, I have forgotten.

All these people came to Gatsby's house in the summer.

Generalized time could hardly be more specific than it is here. Names are named. The names not only substitute for description, they sprout verbs of casual gaudiness and move on. This is not scenic—lists are quite different from scenes—it conveys the serial quality of repeated time. Brightness of detail, ever important for Fitzgerald, is given full freedom here, and the rhythm of an unrolled list convinces us that time ran on and on.

What does it say about readers' expectations if the maneuvers of time in *Gatsby* can feel "classic"? It would seem that we expect stories to come in close for the key points and get to the next spots with all due haste. We're impatient modern readers and we want the immediacy of scene. Movies have helped build this hunger in us, but not only movies. As readers, as audience, we want to directly hear what people are saying, we want to see their faces while they're saying it—we want intimacy with the characters. (At least in realistic fiction.) And we want a sense of destination. *Gatsby* wins its classic status, I think, by its neatly drafted economy, its concentrated scenes and sneaky methods of summary. And everything is kept moving, through the scenes' degree of inflection—the stream of events is always rising to reach a point. By the end, Gatsby's been killed, Daisy has chosen Tom, Nick has decided what to make of it all, nothing more can happen. This is fictional time, where events play out and possibilities are exhausted, so that meaning can emerge.

Long Time

Compressing time is what all fiction does—it's very rare that the words on the page correspond to real time. We're told life is short but art is long, but life in its daily form takes up more time. An exact transcript of a simple everyday conversation would go on for pages. Writers are always trying to contain an unruly mass, to get time trimmed to fit within borders.

A beautiful example of quite short fiction that deals with decades is Anton Chekhov's "The Darling" (1899). No more than ten pages long, it has the artless economy of a master's later work. At the onset, Olga is a young girl with a genuinely tender, sweet nature. She adores those she loves and echoes their opinions. Happily married to the manager of a theater, she speaks of nothing but how the box office loses money every time it rains and the public doesn't appreciate high art. Her husband is delighted with her, but he dies suddenly, on a trip to Moscow, and she is plunged into bitter mourning. She emerges only when a lumberyard owner takes an interest, and soon all of her conversations are about the cost of shipping timber. Her second marriage is also happy— waiting only for the blessing of children—but after six years this husband dies. For a long time she barely leaves the house, until one day she's heard saying there's no proper animal inspection in town. People guess that she's having an affair with the local veterinary surgeon, secret because he still has a wife, who's left him and taken their child. When he's sent to another district, Olga is desolate and lonely for years. Her plump-cheeked prettiness fades with age. Only when the veterinary surgeon returns—this time with his wife and young son—does Olga find a new joy in taking care of the often neglected son. She is heard in town complaining that the school gives much too much homework. This is her last attachment, and it's a sadder one because the boy is just old enough to resent being adored.

Olga's fate is to do the same thing over and over—that's all she knows. Sometimes this works and sometimes it doesn't. Her habit of devotion (Tolstoy much admired this and found her "marvelous and holy") gives her two happy marriages but is less welcome to later objects of affection. How can a story be about a character who doesn't change? Chekhov's solution is to have the situation change around her—a perfect reason to use a long time span. The structure of the story is a series. It takes three to make a series, since two of anything might be just a coincidence. A series of repeated acts is the pattern of jokes: a dog walks into a bar, and the first time, he says . . . and the second time, he says . . . The third time is the punch line. In folktales and fables, the series of three is a clear form of narrative argument.

"The Darling" has quite a lot of summary in it. Olga goes from being young and adorable to old and plain, and the story has to evoke that in a few pages. Chekhov has designed the story to get us swiftly to the melancholy of the closing. His trick is to render summary as if it were scene. When he's describing a repeated action, it's as if it were happening just this once in front of us. Even his summarizing language falls into a list of specifics:

> It seemed to her that she had been in the timber trade for ages and ages, and that the most important and necessary thing in life was timber; and there was something intimate and touching to her in the very sound of such words as "balk," "post," "pole," "beam," "scantling," "batten," "lath," "plank," etc.

Thus even in a story that leaps over long spans of time there's the intimacy of the close gaze.

We can hear Olga's pleasure in appropriating the words. It's worth noting the lightness of Chekhov's touch here; he opts for a list rather than a speech, keeping the emphasis on what Olga feels. Contemporary writers are often strongly attracted to jargon, to the great specialized vocabulary of a trade or age group or class. Chekhov's concreteness is selective, and seemingly casual and by the by, to give him the speed he wants.

"The Darling" is simple, tight, and brief, but there is also a tradition of the novelistic long story that stretches over years of fictional events—a story that is stuffed with time and characters. A long, complicated story with an extended time frame is happy to ignore what Edgar Allan Poe called "the single effect." Without depending on a single galvanizing scene, it can amble along and look at change that comes about through years of underground accretion and zigzagging routes of causation. It can be like a novel, only shorter—a hybrid form with its own virtues.

In narrating a life story, a straight chronology is the most basic approach. Flaubert is the master of this, as seen in his classic long story of a Breton peasant, "A Simple Heart" (1877). As a young man, Flaubert originally wanted to write lushly detailed narratives with exotic historical settings (an enthusiasm he later returned to in *Salammbô*), and in "The Simple Heart" I've always loved the way his instinct for gorgeous details gets channeled into the plain story of a "simple" woman. We first meet the servant Félicité in her indistinct later years:

> Her face was thin and her voice was sharp. At twenty-
> five she was often taken for forty; once she reached

fifty, she stopped looking any age in particular. Always
silent and upright and deliberate in her movements,
she looked like a wooden doll driven by clock-work.

This picture is prologue. The real action begins in
Félicité's adolescence, with her first instance of devotion:
"Like everyone else, she had her love-story." Flaubert
marches in a straight line from this point on, but not in a
steady cadence; his art is to know where to linger, where
to speed up. He lingers, as we might expect, in moments
of high emotion or key dramatic interplay or in settings
that leave a strong impression on Félicité: her employer's
haut bourgeois decor, the church where she takes her
employer's daughter Virginie for catechism. Supplying
close sensory detail came easily to Flaubert—no one
could have done it better—and for many writers this
is the "easy part," the skill they've been most taught to
practice. The tricky part is conveying the passage of
years in such a short space. A lifetime has to pass in a
thirty-nine-page story.

One vital technique is to render habitual action as if
it were a single scene:

> To "occupy her mind," she asked if her nephew Victor
> might come and see her, and permission was granted.
>
> He used to arrive after Mass on Sunday, his
> cheeks flushed, his chest bare, and smelling of the

countryside through which he had come. She laid a
place for him straight away, opposite hers, and they
had lunch together. Eating as little as possible herself,
in order to save the expense, she stuffed him so full of
food that he fell asleep after the meal. When the first
bell for vespers rang, she woke him up, brushed his
trousers, tied his tie, and set off for church, leaning
on his arm with all a mother's pride.

And Victor's later months at sea are conveyed thus:

On sunny days she hoped he was not too thirsty, and
when there was a storm she was afraid he would be
struck by lightning. Listening to the wind howling in
the chimney or blowing slates off the roof, she saw
him being buffeted by the very same storm, perched
on the top of a broken mast, with his whole body
bent backwards under a sheet of foam; or again—and
these were reminiscences of the illustrated geography
book—he was being eaten by savages, captured by
monkeys in a forest, or dying on a desert shore.

No images could be more vivid, and yet we have the
sense of endless (and obsessive) repetition. Flaubert's
summaries are fuller than Chekhov's quick strokes, and
less static than Fitzgerald's glittering lists. They are sum-

maries that unfold in sequence like scenes—they are quite a lot like scenes, but aren't scenes.

Flaubert moves over decades, sometimes with flat-footed directness ("Then the years slipped by, each one like the last, with nothing to vary the rhythm of the great festivals"), but most effectively through details of physical change and decay. Félicité and her employer come across a hat—"made of plush with a long nap; but the moths had ruined it"—once worn by the now-dead Virginie. And no reader ever forgets the description of the last days of Félicité's stuffed parrot, the once-glorious Loulou:

> Although the parrot was not a corpse, the worms were eating him up. One of his wings was broken, and the stuffing was coming out of his stomach. But she was blind by now, and she kissed him on the forehead and pressed him against her cheek.

The reader has seen Félicité go from a brisk and vigorous girl to a blind and disordered invalid. (Note how image does the work here that incident sometimes does in the novel.) And what is perhaps most striking is the way Flaubert has organized a shaped story out of what he keeps telling us is a plodding and uneventful narrative. His method, despite the story's own disclaimers, has been to suggest a pattern. The markers in the plot are Félicité's serial objects of devotion: her employer's young daughter, her own nephew, and at last her pet parrot, alive and dead. Their worthiness is never the point; Félicité's own form of a religious temperament is the point, as the final transformation of the parrot into the Holy Ghost tells us.

"A Simple Heart" supports the premise that long time is best narrated by summary functioning as if it were scene. And a short story (even a forty-page one) trying to contain a lifetime can surely use the compression summary gives. But as I looked again at fondly remembered examples, I was startled to notice that novels—with their chapters and sections, their room to stroll—can sometimes opt to avoid the convenient speed of summary.

I have a lifelong fondness for what are sometimes called chronicle novels, straightforward tales that resemble fictionalized biographies. In a chronicle novel, a central character is young at the beginning and old at the end, and this elemental contrast is crucial to what lingers in the mind when the book is put down. No conflict is more vivid in such fiction than the changes wrought by time. Contemporary examples include V. S. Naipaul's *A House for Mr. Biswas*, Jhumpa Lahiri's *The*

Namesake, and Carol Shields's *The Stone Diaries.* Some of the best writers in this form deliberately choose quite ordinary characters with unstriking experiences, and this tradition goes back to the nineteenth century. Novels of this sort have to work to avoid the sin of dullness, while deliberately avoiding the rise and fall of a single dominating drama. The challenge for these writers is to make the march of mundane events compelling and to cause them to add up to a sum total with emotional resonance beyond anything we could have guessed. I may have first been drawn to such books as a young writer because—like the nineteenth-century realists who polemicized against the artificial—I liked the idea that fiction could be made out of unspectacular materials.

A stubbornly favorite book of mine for years was Arnold Bennett's *The Old Wives' Tale* (1908). The very title had a defiant prissiness to it that I liked. In his introduction, Bennett describes watching a "ridiculous" old woman in a Parisian restaurant and musing on the "extreme pathos in the mere fact" that she was once young. He resolves to write a novel about the "history" of some unexceptional woman, inspired by the great example of Guy de Maupassant's *Une Vie* (in English the title is *A Woman's Life*). He decides to "'go one better' than *Une Vie*" by focusing on two women rather than one. Bennett's tale of two English sisters— one stays home in the provinces, one runs off to Paris with a man she thinks she loves—is a mosaic of small details, deepened by its moments of transcendent intimacy with its characters. What I learned from it as a struggling first-novelist was that details of private sensation could do a great deal of work if they were truly exact and surprising, that it was possible to stay in scene even in a very long narrative, and that an episodic plot could be lit by passages of vision.

Here's the end of a scene, two-thirds through *The Old Wives' Tale,* in which the sister Sophia, who's been abandoned by her caddish husband, enjoys a rare and giddy dinner out during the siege of Paris (four bad months during the Franco-Prussian War) and is offered a new start by a very decent Frenchman named Chirac:

> She did not love him. But she was moved. And she wanted to love him. She wanted to yield to him, only liking him, and to love afterwards. But this obstinate instinct held her back.
>
> "I do not say, now," Chirac went on. "Let me hope."
>
> The Latin theatricality of his gestures and his tone made her sorrowful for him.
>
> . . . She drew her face away from his, firmly. She was not hard, not angry now. Disconcerted by her compassion, he loosed her.
>
> "My poor Chirac," she said. . . .

They left the restaurant silently, with a foolish air.

Dusk was falling on the mournful streets, and the lamplighters were lighting the miserable oil lamps that had replaced gas. They two, and the lamplighters, and an omnibus were alone in the streets. The gloom was awful; it was desolating. The universal silence seemed to be the silence of despair. Steeped in woe, Sophia thought wearily upon the hopeless problem of existence. For it seemed to her that she and Chirac had created this woe out of nothing, and yet it was an incurable woe!

In lesser hands, this citing of the "universal" could be too washy—could become a bit of rhetoric that invokes the cosmos in the service of sentiment—but Bennett is such a prosy writer, so in love with hard facts, that this sudden widening can be judiciously beautiful. Experience, for Bennett, is always a composite of details (this is why Virginia Woolf mocked him for reducing character to lists of social externals) and his goal in *The Old Wives' Tale* is to unflinchingly evoke the proverbial sense of life as one thing after another, to write a plot so uninflected that minor events take up as much room as major ones, and yet to elevate this to art. He relies on the solemn, modest strength of lyrically heightened moments, spots where the ordinary is sublimely lit, where a character's interior eloquence gathers events into poignancy.

As it happened, I didn't need Arnold Bennett to point me to the novels of Maupassant—I'd grown up reading them in my family's library, thrilled by their hardheaded treatment of romance and illusion. *A Woman's Life*, one of Maupassant's least glamorous books, first published in 1883, follows Jeanne, a gently bred girl in Normandy, from the day she leaves her convent school, eager and dreamy, through a bad marriage, an ungrateful son, and a penniless widowhood. Like Bennett after him, Maupassant works almost entirely in scene. Maupassant's pacing is less regular—he covers just six years in the first three-quarters of the novel and glides through decades in the last quarter—a sign, probably, of a more well made plot. But he too works through mundane particulars; a lifetime is rendered through flashes of sensory detail.

A Woman's Life is a harsh book—more modern and austere than Bennett's—and has its own lessons to teach about handling long spells of time. Its characters are villainous, wily, or helpless; we are more often horrified or exasperated by them than weeping for them. The best sides of the heroine's mild nature—and her most joyous moments—are in her responsiveness to nature. At the onset, a very young Jeanne looks out her bedroom window at the sea, and "in the soft brilliance of the night she was conscious of mysterious shivers, a palpitating sense of undefined hopes like a breath of happiness." Her somewhat delayed sexual awakening happens in the lush outdoor setting of a rustic honeymoon, and, conversely, the most violent scene in the book involves a hysterical priest's rage against the sexuality of the natural world.

This pointing to nature is actually key in the handling of fictional time. The plot, considered by itself, would seem to be merely grim and cynical and drily pathetic. Nor is the story punctuated by the characters' lucid insights. We would drown in their details were it not for the unsentimental evocation of endless seasons of wet dirt and regrowth, of larger enveloping forces. Jeanne's life (all bad luck and foolish fragility) is not tragic because it is drawn as what might be called "sustainable"—part of a replenishing order. When Jeanne, in late middle age, with everything lost, passionately greets her abandoned grandchild with smothering kisses, her bossy servant warns,

> "Come! Come! Madame Jeanne, that's enough! You'll make her scream."
>
> Then she added, no doubt in answer to her own thoughts: "You see, life is never as good or as bad as one thinks."

This is the line that closes the novel, and it is an argument for the chronicle novel itself, with its insistence on the impact of serial events over the long haul.

In *The Old Wives' Tale* and *A Woman's Life,* long-time-passing is the substitute for high action: duration gives weight to the quotidian. A much larger scale of suffering awaits Fugui, the hero of *To Live,* a novel by the Chinese writer Yu Hua, first published in 1993 in China and in the United States in translation in 2003. In 1994 it was made into a stunning movie, directed by Zhang Yimou, with Gong Li cast as the long-suffering wife. The book has a frame—the alleged author is an unnamed young man going through the countryside collecting folk songs—but almost all of it is told in the first person by one remarkable character he meets, the aged Fugui, a man who has been through everything.

First person allows for skipping and jumping and pausing in the narrative. Fugui is an impressionistic narrator, quick with the pithy detail; his first sketch of provincial prosperity dwells on his wealthy father's eccentric fondness for shitting in the out-of-doors. In Fugui's spoiled youth as a silk-clad rich kid, he gambles away the entire family fortune and with devastating speed is reduced to hardscrabble farming. This reversal is only the first step in his saga. While he's walking through town, he's conscripted by the Nationalist army, threatened and starved and thrown into combat, and captured and freed by the Communists. He returns home in time to see his old gambling rival, the man who took over his family mansion, now being executed as a "despotic landlord."

Much more awaits (we are only a quarter of the way through)—poverty, family illness, violent government policies. Fugui's hard-won survival skills sometimes mislead him. He often does the thing he should have done the last time, and it's dead wrong this time. Scared of displeasing anyone in power, after the atrocities he's seen, and eager for his son to be more than a farmer, after his own years of hard work and hard luck, Fugui forces the boy to go to school, where (as it turns out) he is in much more danger than at home.

The flow of time is channeled by a strong and personable narrating voice, frank and sometimes comic. We never forget that we are being told this story by the principal character in it. The first-person narrator has the economy of direct commentary ("When Fengxia [his daughter] moved to town it felt like our spirits had gone with her"). And any broad statement Fugui makes is apt to melt at once into an illustrating scene. Here's a descripton of his daughter, left mute and deaf by childhood illness, after she's newly married. In a very natural flow, the summary of how her neighbors feel is followed by bits of concrete action:

[The] neighbors took a real fancy to Fengxia [his daughter]. As soon as I'd get there they'd all compliment her by saying how hardworking and intelligent she was. Once she started sweeping she'd sweep the ground in front of her neighbors' houses—hell, once she got going, she'd sweep half the street. Seeing Fengxia beginning to break a sweat, the neighbors would go over and pat her on the back to tell her to stop. Only then would she go back inside with a bright smile on her face.

Yu Hua seems miraculously able to avoid the kind of prose designated as "transition"; the book seems never to have to tell us that years passed between this and that. It is so packed with events that one episode arises immediately after another. Time is relentless; no need for any white space here. By the end of the book, Fugui has lost everyone in his life—son, daughter, wife, son-in-law, grandson. His one companion is his faithful old ox, whom he calls Fugui. He spurs it on by the trick of calling out the names of imaginary oxen working hard beside it, names that are in fact the names of his dead family. The book ends with the two Fuguis—man and ox—going off into the sunset together, watched by the young witness who's heard the whole story.

It is true that this technique might be a disaster in the hands of a lesser writer. Events packed together could feel scrambled and could numb us with their density.

I would say that the reason for Yu Hua's success is not only technical mastery but—to use an imprecise but necessary term—his depth. For all its simplicity of tone, this is an ambitious book about the fluctuating ironies of history and the extreme suffering attached to them, so the rush of events has weight. The balance between the comically trivial and the unspeakably painful is part of the book's beauty.

To Live, as its title suggests, is about survival, and the plot piles one obstacle on another; no character could be more overloaded than Fugui. The long time span is essential to our appreciation of Fugui's achievement in staying alive. (Fugui says a neighbor has called him and the ox "a couple of old bastards that just won't die.")

Yu Hua has said that he was inspired to write *To Live* after hearing the "American folk song" "Old Black Joe"—"about an elderly black slave who experienced a life's worth of hardships . . . yet he still looked upon the world with eyes of kindness, offering not the slightest complaint." Yu Hua can hardly be blamed for not knowing the song was written by Stephen Foster, a white guy from Pittsburgh—Yu's point is that endurance of a certain kind is moving to contemplate. Stirred by a lyric, he clearly saw how the chronicle novel was the supremely suitable form for such contemplation.

If *To Live* is a book with almost no white space between events, Evan Connell's *Mrs. Bridge* is a novel whose methods make the freest possible use of pauses—white spaces of rest, silence, no comment—between events. The book, first published in 1959 (and followed by *Mr. Bridge* in 1969), traces the life of a middle-class wife and mother in Kansas City in the decades before World War II. It is written in very short chapters, some no more than a few paragraphs, some four or five pages long, each in brightly terse prose with the concentrated force of a short-short story. These episodes often consist of small household dilemmas; Mrs. Bridge has hungers for a fuller life but is most often seen fending off whatever force unsettles her. Connell's authorial voice is not afraid to mock (gently and otherwise) his characters' panicked attachments to convention. But the originality of his method is in the way each chapter is a distinct modular unit, with its own mini-conclusion, as if Mrs. Bridge has convinced herself each time that she's solved the problem. She cannot, of course, always escape her own disquiet.

Here's one of the shorter chapters:

On a winter morning not long after one of these excursions Mrs. Bridge happened to come upon Douglas [her son] in the sewing room; he was standing quietly with his hands clasped behind his back and his head bent slightly to one side. So adult did he look in the depth of his meditation that she could not resist smiling. Then she saw that he was staring at the dummy of her figure. She had kept the dummy there near the sewing machine for a long time and had supposed that no one in the family paid any attention to it, but after this particular day—unless she was using it to make herself a dress—the dummy stood behind an up-ended trunk in the attic.

Life—Mrs. Bridge insists and fears—can be led only in small, manageable chunks of experience, one narrow bit at a time. The short, clipped chapters are designed to evoke this. As readers, we get a larger view of her life than Mrs. Bridge does.

Connell's stylized approach to the novel more or less saves him from the problem of transitions or summary. He gets to bring down the curtain in a flash and move right to the next scene. Occasionally, Mrs. Bridge reminisces for us, or the narrative indulges in quick swipes through time. ("That was the year Ruth finally managed to graduate from high school.") Sentences like that are hard to avoid. Even the skillful Maupassant resorts now and then to "Nothing else happened until the last days of July," or "Two uneventful years passed peacefully," but like Connell he gets himself back into scene as fast as he can.

One lesson I found myself taking from these novels is how writers as different as Bennett, Maupassant, Yu, and Connell all are able to stay in scene, despite the great swathes of time they are leaping through. I don't happen to think scene is innately superior to every other approach (some people do, but I don't); my point is rather that surprisingly little is needed *between* scenes to keep time running along. To judge from the success of these books, readers can keep up just fine with a pace of shorter scenes, and lots of such scenes, and can accept the illusion of whole lifetimes passing as readily as they accept the more familiar illusion of a season or a year in a novel.

Before we leave long time in fiction, I want to seize the chance to look at what Virginia Woolf so eccentrically and emphatically does in the section of *To the Lighthouse* titled "Time Passes." Her achievement is—among other things—to cover a long span of time ("seven years," her journal says) *without* using either scene or summary. It is a technical tour de force, a very daring fictional strategy.

After *To the Lighthouse* spends a long, rich, complicated summer day inside the heads of a range of characters staying at the Ramsays' country house in the Hebrides, "Time Passes" begins with characters looking out into the darkening horizon—"'One can hardly tell which is the sea and which is the land,' said Prue"—and going off to bed. Once they're asleep, "nothing stirred in the drawing-room or on the staircase. Only through the rusty hinges and swollen sea-moistened woodwork certain airs, detached from the body of the wind (the house was ramshackle after all) crept round corners and ventured indoors." We've left the clock time of daily events and entered into deeper time, beyond any individual consciousness. The human scale of events occurs in brackets: "[Mr. Ramsay, stumbling along a passage one dark morning, stretched his arms out, but Mrs. Ramsay having died rather suddenly the night before, his arms, though stretched out, remained empty.]"

The reader's shock at this news is met only with further reports of the house's abandonment and visitation by dust, echoes, light, damp. The actions of decay are abstract: "So loveliness reigned and stillness, and together made the shape of loveliness itself, a form from which life had parted." Around this unobserved space—like a forest with no one to hear a tree fall—unnamed mortals ask their eternal questions ("What am I?" "What is this?"). News of the Ramsay entourage comes briefly, in brackets—Prue Ramsay has her wedding, Prue Ramsay dies in childbirth, Andrew Ramsay is killed in a battle in France, Mr. Carmichael publishes a book of poems.

A conflict (to use a workshop term) is stirring between the "insensibility of nature"—what does it care about the Ramsays?—and a rallied resistance against the drift to death. ("If the feather had fallen, if it had tipped the scale downwards, the whole house would have plunged to the depths to lie upon the sands of oblivion.")

It is expressed in terms of housekeeping (as in Marilynne Robinson's novel *Housekeeping,* with the same thematic tilt), and Woolf speaks well of the homely efforts made by the servants, their bustling with soap and sun, so that her major characters can return to the house, the action can begin again.

It should be said that Woolf's chorus of human questioners ("Will you fade? Will you perish?"), waking to walk by the sea, are pointing also to something exalted in the chaos. What makes the sleepers so restless is an intuition of the eternal, a half-understood knowledge they can just barely glimpse and bring back into ordinary time. Underneath much of the novel is the pull of such efforts, the frustration and exhilaration.

What can be learned from what Woolf does in *To the Lighthouse?* Before beginning it, Woolf said in her diary that she wanted to write "this impersonal thing, which I'm dared to do by my friends, the flight of time and the consequent break in my design. That passage (I conceive the book in three parts . . .) interests me very much." The novelist who pioneered a fiction of consciousness sets herself to convey time without consciousness. To report "this impersonal thing" she has to posit an insubstantial observer, an eye without a head. Less human than your basic omniscient narrator, a voice that's incantatory yet distinctly modern. Perhaps what we can take from Woolf is a reminder of the freedom available, the purity of boldness, the triumph of a dare taken. Woolf is both direct—she tackles "time passing" head-on—and defiantly subtle and ornate. She plays with scale, something fiction is good at doing, and she uses all her powers, truly stretches them to the limit, to convey the tidal pull of time, the story under the story.

Switchback Time

In any conversation about film, people are apt to hear themselves refer to the *backstory*. Without exactly knowing where we learned it, we all use the word to mean the stuff in the past that's fueling the current story. It is those bits from characters' histories that explain the cravings, fears, and affinities that run the present-time plot. *Flashback* is an older term for this, often referring to sudden scenic shifts into remembered time. First we're with a prisoner on death row, then we're with a boy being scolded by his father. *Flashback* has slightly tacky connotations; it has been abused too often, used glibly to supply a too-simple cause and effect for motivation.

Switchback time suggests a more complicated sort of design. I'm using it to mean a zigzag movement back and forth among time frames, the method of a fiction that alternates different "eras" (like the deliberate swing of a mountain road that carries us this way and that when a straight line can't do it). This story design uses the shifts in an order that doesn't give dominance to a particular time. *Then* and *now* and *further back* are all partners with an investment in the outcome. Their separate roles are essential to the point the story is making; one isn't a footnote to the other. Any writer who has struggled to include all the strands of material attached to an initial notion will see the attractions of this scheme. Alice Munro is our strongest contemporary exponent of this method.

Munro's art is in the effect of shifting perspectives. Any assumption or emotional certainty always has its unanticipated corrections (for both character and reader), and time shifts are needed to show this. For instance, in "A Real Life" (from *Open Secrets*), the rough and unglamorous neighbor who shoots a feral cat becomes the bride in shining satin of a wealthy Australian (trumping a much more likely candidate) and later still the settled wife who writes home to Canada, "I have grown as fat as the Queen of Tonga." Our notions of who gets married and why, and what married life is, are interrupted and regrouped several times in this piece.

In a story like "The Progress of Love" (from Munro's 1986 collection of the same title) we start with a phone call from the narrator's father announcing her mother's death, and go to a bouquet of backstories about the mother, the mother's mother, and the narrator as a child and much later as a dating divorcée. Love's "progress" through generations has involved a series of variant interpretations of one incident.

Old actions keep getting new labels, much as the narrator, grandly christened Euphemia, after her grandmother, now goes by the name Fame. Everything looks different when it is seen from a different angle of telling, a different point in time and knowledge. At the core of "Progress of Love" is a story recounted by Fame's mother from her childhood: her own depressed mother, anguished at her husband's infidelity, stands on a chair with a rope around her neck and says, "Go and get your father." But Fame also remembers a long-ago visit from her aunt Beryl, who arrives with a different, lighter version of the same story—"she could carry a joke too far."

And Aunt Beryl is horrified to hear that Fame's pious mother once indignantly burnt the stack of cash that was a legacy from her father, the alleged philanderer. Throw out good money just for a grudge? Fame's father, who seems not to have known about this cash-burning, supports his wife by saying, "It was her money, Beryl." The older Fame (who's told her own half-invented version of the incident) is later sure that her father's defense of her mother is the most important part of all of it, though no one else will see it that way. At the story's close, Fame—on her own since fifteen, divorced, self-supporting, modern—contemplates her own fluctuating life with its many restarts, its sharp contrast to the older world with its fixity of bonds and resentments:

> I wonder if those moments [of kindness] aren't more
> valued, and deliberately gone after, in the setups
> some people like myself have now, than they were

in those old marriages, where love and grudges could
be growing underground, so confused and stubborn,
it must have seemed they had forever.

In the most successful of Munro's stories, there's a
particular glory in sensing the story's order at the end,
feeling the ways in which—to use the metaphor Munro
herself has employed—the different parts are different rooms in one house. Her shuffled sequence forces
incomplete recognitions; our ideas get unraveled and
corrected. There's always a center, but we have to move
around to see it.

Munro's method is to jump over gaps in time. It
has been said that she doesn't write novels because she
doesn't like to fill in the between-times. She once said
that the novel had to have a coherence that she no longer saw in the lives around her (by now she has stopped
having to make such excuses). But such a statement
does suggest how the sprawl of these stories involves,
in fact, an economy of means.

Munro is careful to always supply markers, so we
know where we are in time: "I got a call at work, and
it was my father. This was not long after I was divorced
and started in the real-estate office. Both of my boys
were in school." Or: "In the summer of 1947, when I was
twelve, I helped my mother paper the downstairs bedroom, the spare room. My mother's sister, Beryl, was
coming to see us." The texturing details, supplied with

seeming casualness, keep us grounded; there's never any dreaminess about where we are.

Munro's work in the 1990s involved brilliant uses of historical material and dazzling sweeps of time. The librarian in "Carried Away" (from *Open Secrets*, 1994) is first seen getting letters from a soldier in World War I and last seen as a prosperous matron of the 1950s. In the complex and ambitious "The Albanian Virgin" (also from *Open Secrets*) Munro spins two plot lines, set in different times. In the remote mountains of northern Albania, a young woman is kidnapped by a tribal group and learns to live among them, first doing women's tasks and then taking on the gender-crossing role of a "Virgin," a lone shepherdess who dresses as a man and is excused from marrying. These adventures are told from a hospital bed by an elderly eccentric named Charlotte, speaking to her friend Claire, a bookstore owner, who (we don't find out until two-thirds of the way through the story) has fled her own broken marriage and the lover who helped break it. Charlotte at first declares she's making up the Albanian story, but we assume it's her experience and she later says the incidents are "from life."

Much of our initial attention in this story is on the exoticism of the Albanian material:

> There, with great ceremony and delight, they shaved
> off the hair above her forehead. Then they combed

some black, bubbling dye through the hair that remained. The dye was greasy—the hair became so stiff that they could shape it into wings and buns as firm as blood puddings. Everybody thronged about, criticizing and admiring.

Munro has included a wild abundance of ethnological details. At one point in Claire's part of the story, Charlotte's husband, Gjurdhi, tries to sell old books— *A Trek through the Black Peaks, High Albania, Secret Lands of Southern Europe*—that are clearly Munro's research list (my reissued copy of *High Albania* has a photo of an Albanian Virgin). The reader is apt to get so happily lost in the melodrama of Albanian captivity that only the rhythm of the two plots implies their final connection. Claire's long, interesting, risky period of singlehood is ended when her lover comes to claim her in her bookstore, and the young woman kidnapped in High Albania is met in Trieste by the tall, dark, grouchy Franciscan who's helped her escape. The exquisite strangeness of both women's unanchored, unsorted solitude is over, and they are folded into the form of the couple.

By working in switchback time, Munro is resisting—successfully—the limits of seeing a story from a single point in time. Lottar, the adventurous girl who's marooned in the mountains of Albania, is also Charlotte, the wry, tawdry old lady in a western Canadian city who steals books. The two exist as figures drawn with comparable fullness. Claire, the single woman eating a baked potato for supper in her kitchen, is also the long-married mother of two who is telling us all this. Her own summing up is full of erasures and revisions:

> *We have been very happy.*
> *I have often felt completely alone.*
> *There is always in this life something to discover.*
> *The days and the years have gone by in some sort*
>   *of blur.*
> *On the whole, I am satisfied.*

It strikes me that switchback time—used with dazzling craft in stories like "The Albanian Virgin"—is also a natural method of oral storytelling at its best. People are always interrupting themselves, often to excellent purpose. One of my favorite examples of this is from an essay that Francis Steegmuller, best known as a critic and translator of Flaubert, published in the *New Yorker* in 1964. Steegmuller lived for many years in southern Italy with his wife, the novelist Shirley Hazzard. The essay, "Ciao, Fabrizio," begins with his seeing what he thinks is a wedding party in a restaurant near Amalfi. The lovely young bride is tearful, perhaps because she is marrying "an ageless little clerk," and at one point is led away, quietly sobbing, by her mother. The evening ends with celebratory fireworks over the harbor and the phrase CIAO ADRIANA / CIAO FABRIZIO on a great glowing signboard in the night sky.

The following afternoon the author discovers from his friend's cook, Maria, that what he saw was not the wedding at all—no, Maria has just been to the actual wedding earlier today—he has misunderstood everything. In order to explain, Maria asks permission to tell another story. In Naples, street construction uncovered an ancient catacomb containing bones and skulls on rock shelves. People of the neighborhood became devoted to caring for the bones: "Each person, you might say, *adopted* the skull he or she chose, and sometimes gave it a name, and some people put glass bells over their skulls with labels on them to keep them free from dust." People knelt on cushions next to their skulls, murmured tenderly to them. No one cared whether the skulls were pagan or Christian—"They're all *morti,* and the *morti* all deserve our prayers and love, because they were once just like us."

The narrator still doesn't get it, and Maria finally gives him the key piece of information: Fabrizio is not the groom at all, but the bride's dead brother, killed as a child during the war. The fireworks he saw were to remember and salute the dead boy at the time of his sister's wedding. It was entirely suitable and seemly and necessary to the family—and the bride—to make a great display of love for their own *morto* at this time. How could they forget him?

Maria might have revealed this fact before—her intervening tale doesn't help the narrator guess a thing. What the tale does is make him understand what the fireworks and the bride's tears mean. The instructive surprise in this (to writers) is that Maria doesn't pick an episode about the bride's family as her explanatory vehicle, which would have been the more obvious choice. Steegmuller says that Maria, who is "only fairly literate . . . nonetheless possesses an unusual ability to see events in larger contexts." What the switchback tale to the catacombs does is to provide this largeness, to give the material not only its cultural frame but also its legitimate depth. What might be a merely charming story about those crazy Neapolitans is instead an illustration of the lasting footprint of death and the beauty of human responses to it.

Switchback time, though it makes a story more complicated, is as elemental as the process of associative thought. It is most useful when an added line of event can really clarify and expand what a story is about. No story could carry this argument further and deeper than my last example, James Baldwin's much loved and much anthologized story "Sonny's Blues" (published in 1957, and then in the 1965 collection *Going to Meet the*

Man). The event that sets everything in motion is the arrest of the narrator's younger brother, Sonny, on a heroin charge. The opening line still sounds majestic to me, after years of reading and teaching this story: "I read about it in the paper, in the subway, on my way to work." The action stays there for a few pages—with the narrator, a high school teacher in Harlem, talking to a neighborhood junkie in the schoolyard—and then there's a time leap and a few lines of summary, flat in tone and terrible in content: "And I didn't write Sonny or send him anything for a long time. When I finally did, it was just after my little girl died, he wrote me back a letter which made me feel like a bastard."

Most of the story takes place after Sonny, a talented jazz pianist, is let out of prison. He stays with the narrator and his wife and kids, and he settles back into the world, watched warily by his brother. But the narrator, in his tense and loving consideration of Sonny, moves into other key time frames. The first is a memory of his mother telling him, "Your Daddy once had a brother. . . . You didn't never know that, did you?" This lost brother was killed on a nighttime highway in the South, by a car of drunken white men whose joking went wrong. The second is a memory of arguing with Sonny as a piano-obsessed teenager. And the last, most important switchback tells about the narrator's daughter Grace: "she only lived a little over two years. She died of polio and she suffered." The account of her death cuts to the bone and makes me tearful no matter how many times I've read it, and a crucial turn follows: "I think I may have written Sonny the very day that little Grace was buried. I was sitting in the living room in the dark, by myself, and I suddenly thought of Sonny. My trouble made his real."

The rest of the story shows the narrator trying to know Sonny more truly, and there is an exquisite, triumphant last scene of Sonny at the piano in a club. Sonny's music—the blues, uncovered and improvised—is the coda to a story whose use of switchback is an argument for the crucial need to connect time lines, a story in which a character learns to listen to his brother only because fate led him on his own separate path through the unbearable. *My trouble made his real.*

I have sometimes asked students to imagine what the story would be if Baldwin had chosen to have Sonny tell it, a point of view that would seem to be the more obvious choice. The title identifies it as Sonny's blues, after all, and I'd say Sonny has a more interesting life—addiction, jail, creative struggle. The narrator is the stodgy schoolteacher who gets married as soon as he comes out of the army and who worries that Sonny will never make a living with that piano stuff. I think of Flannery O'Connor's famous pronouncement (from "On Her Own Work" in *Mystery and Manners*) that "violence is strangely capable of returning my characters to reality and preparing them to accept their moment of grace. Their heads are so hard that almost nothing else will do the work." The narrator of "Sonny's Blues" (though he's kinder and more honest than most of O'Connor's characters) is in such a situation. The knock that almost kills him—the loss of little Grace—allows him to hear Sonny, to take in what he's been deaf to.

Sometimes students argue that Sonny, the junkie, would just make a mess of telling his story, an assumption directly contrary to every bit of evidence in the story: Sonny is plenty self-aware and "articulate" (a word whose condescension in praise of African American men has already been pointed out in our political life). Baldwin, with the skill to handle any viewpoint—he made a white racist the central consciousness in "Going to Meet the Man"—surely would have had no trouble making Sonny the teller. Sonny's story, told by Sonny, could have worked fine. But Baldwin was after something else: the depth of understanding that only a resonance of time frames could bring about.

Slowed Time

Aristotle in the *Poetics* claimed that superior plots tended to involve "discovery," the bit of truth dredged from a character's past that changes everything now. It is also the method of detective stories and spy novels—the plot has to let the protagonist dig around to find what's gone before.

The authors who use switchback time to great effect are masters at just such digging. But, in fact, many writers are entirely happy to do without backstory. Ernest Hemingway and Raymond Carver, for instance, are not much given to it and can keep pretty strictly within the present moment. Carver is especially adept at citing an often weighty past with a glancing reference. In "Chef's House" (from *Cathedral*, 1983), the narrator gets a phone call from her ex-husband, who asks her to move in with him again: "He said he was on the wagon." The narrator has fond feelings for her husband, but what she thinks, on hearing this, is, "I knew about that wagon." A novel in one sentence—*I knew about that wagon*—no supporting details needed. We're not going to hear any more about it, either; the cover is pretty much shut on that book. The point of the story at hand is to follow what's left to these characters.

When the past is left out, the focus on the present moment can sometimes lead to the intensity of what I'd call *slowed time.* A very short piece of action is examined very, very closely. Sometimes undergraduates think that this is just what they're in a writing class to be trained to do—to look at a single moment in detail—and there's a lot to be said for this kind of exact close attention. In the wider world of literature, I am sometimes a resistant audience for it because it can seem closer to the lyric impulse (dawdling in the scenery, lingering over a sensation) than to a real narrative urgency. Oh, get on with the story, I may well think.

But remarkable stories have been written in slowed time. One piece of fiction that serves as a sterling example of a very brief moment seen slowly is a short-short story called "The Thirst" by the Egyptian writer Nawal al-Saadawi. (I came across it in an anthology, *Literatures of Asia, Africa, and Latin America,* and it's only four pages long in the close print used by college texts.) In an unnamed Egyptian city, a servant girl has been sent to the market to buy food for her employer. Under the fierce noonday sun, she sees another servant, Hamida, drinking a bottle of ice-cold soda. She can't believe that someone like her can do such a thing—the soda is an unheard-of luxury. Where did Hamida get the money for it? The girl can't stop watching Hamida:

She drank with extreme slowness, moving her fingers
down around the bottle and feeling its coldness with
delight. . . . She lifted it slowly to her mouth and
touched the edge of her lips to the bottle mouth and
licked it, gathering up all the droplets around it with
her tongue; then she raised her arm a bit higher to
tilt the bottle up to her mouth slightly, only allowing
herself a single sip of the rosy, ice-cold liquid. Here
she closed her lips with great control, keeping the sip
in her mouth for a while without swallowing it all at
once; she swallowed it slowly until the last drop of it
disappeared from her mouth.

It's a very voluptuous soda. There's a similarly long description of the narrator's great thirst—it's hot out there
at the market—and her moral deliberation about whether
she's going to cheat her employer out of some money to
buy one of these sodas for herself. If she bargains hard,
if she shaves a little off this purchase and skims a little
off that, she might just have enough. Her mother has told
her never to steal, and her employer will beat her or fire
her if she finds out. She calculates at length the possible
prices of zucchini, tomatoes, and meat. Resourcefulness
and fear battle in her. The story ends with her resolving
to get herself the soda: "the hard slaps could no longer
cause her pain, for she had become used to them, and the
hellfire that burned could no longer frighten her because

it was far away, and the world with all its pains and fears was not equal to a single sip of an ice-cold soda-pop."

What the story shows is two crucial things: the extent to which a very simple action can be broken down into minute stages of sensory detail, and the impact this has in a story. Length is weight in fiction, pretty much. The longer something takes, the more emotionally important it is. In a movie, when the camera pauses over something, we know it's crucial. The danger is in slowing down at the wrong moment—in any fiction, we don't want to hear about savoring a casual cup of coffee that means nothing. In this case, the observed drink of soda is the impetus for profound longing (the story is called "The Thirst"), ethical conflict, and an act that carries real risk.

"The Thirst" is a story of passion—love for a soda makes the supersaturation of detail plausible. A cooler, more distant portrayal of slowed time shows itself, by contrast, in Don DeLillo's "Videotape." Originally published in 1984, the story opens as a flat description of somebody's home video: "It shows a man driving a car. . . . It is just a kid aiming her camera through the rear window of the family car at the windshield of the car behind her." The tape, we are told, is tedious ("It seems to go on forever") and famous, and while we wait for the hinted-at catastrophe to happen, the narrating voice comments: "You know how children with cameras learn to work the exposed moments . . . catching Mom coming out of the bathroom in her cumbrous robe and turbaned towel, looking bloodless and plucked."

In the tape, the man at the wheel is hit by gunfire, while the narrator watches, as he's watched many times before—"You don't usually call your wife over to the TV set. She has her programs, you have yours. But there's a certain urgency here." The man bleeds and dies under the camera's gaze—with the startled jump of the picture and the continued filming serving as signs (the narrator thinks) of the girl's shock and sympathy. We're told that "this is either the tenth or eleventh homicide committed by the Texas Highway Killer" and that the (seemingly random) crimes are committed as if the killer himself were performing something that he expects to see as instant replay. The "awful and unremarkable" event strikes the narrator as an instructional reminder that "every breath you take has two possible endings," and also as a kind of terrible slapstick, the driver as the Poor Soul getting his pie in the face. The final sentences remind us that the television stations are going to keep showing it: "The horror freezes your soul but that doesn't mean that you want them to stop."

This very brief piece might be said to feature characters—the narrator, his wife, Janet, the girl with the camera, the victim, and the offstage killer—and action, the two requirements of conventional narrative. But if its tension and shape rely on the emergence of violence—we do wait to see the killing—the suspense also relies on what the narrator makes of it: we wait to see what he thinks the tape says about us, his fellow viewers and consumers of video culture, as well as what this says about him. The story is memorable for its postmodern layers of perception—we are reading about a guy who is watching a television show of a tape filmed by a kid watching a guy driving a car who is killed.

Once again, slowed time has to do with the importance of the material. The tape is examined by the narrator, as well as by the entire viewing public, in close detail, and has been seen over and over, so that every small point is clear. If coolness in the face of horror is one element of the story, so are implied questions about culpability, voyeurism, sympathy, the morality of publicity: the whole package of what "replay" means.

While al-Saadawi handles time with a straight chronology of immediate sense impressions, followed by a drama of thought, DeLillo does it by alternating between commentary and report, report and commentary: "The way his head is twisted away from the door, the twist of the head gives you only a partial profile and it's the wrong side, it's not the side where he was hit. And maybe you're being a little aggressive here, forcing your wife to watch." All that self-examination on the part of the teller serves to further slow down time. Repetition is part of the experience being narrated— "Hurry up, Janet, here it comes"—the loop keeps running, and the story ends by pointing to us, *hypocrites lecteurs,* who are still watching.

That self-examination on the part of the teller slows down time is why, among other things, many readers resist Proust. At times, I have felt, with some resentment, that my whole life was being slowed down by the activity of reading Proust. I'd been reading for hours, and Proust and I were still in the same spot? My affection for him has sometimes been stronger than my patience.

No discussion of time in fiction can fail to include Proust, whose very title evokes the great paradoxical effort of retrieving lost time, but I am going to isolate just a few factors to look at, take a very quick dip in a vast sea. The critic Richard Howard, in the introduction to the Modern Library edition of *In Search of Lost Time* (the new and more accurate title for *Remembrance of Things Past*), writes a letter directly addressed to Proust: "Often on any one page or in any one passage— somewhere between a chant and a chapter—you [he's addressing Proust] manage to cast your spell, to sound your note, *to tell your truth,* for goodness sake! so that readers don't have to read all the way to the end of the whole book to get what Proust is about."

In one of literary history's most notable manuscript rejections, the Paris publisher Ollendorff wrote to Proust in 1913, "I don't see why a man should take thirty pages to describe how he turns over in bed before he goes to sleep." I'd like to take this complaint as a challenge. It will be instructive, I think, to look at those opening pages for a sense of how slowed time operates in Proust's fiction.

Time, as any experienced fiction reader might well guess, is only slowed outwardly. The narrator, whom we first meet waking from sleep, is having a fiesta of swiftly passing thoughts and memories. We are not in the realm of event, we are in the realm of consciousness. First he's inside whatever book he's been reading, then he's in his own freshly strange bedroom, then he's in a brief memory of childhood, then he's musing over the remnant of a sexual dream, or (we're in habitual time, with variant possibilities) deep sleep throws him into the best waking of all: "I did not even understand in the first moment who I was; I had only, in its original simplicity, the sense of existence as it may quiver in the depths of an animal." And the body itself, in the awkwardness of its sleeping position, unsure of where it finds itself, guesses it is in a place of the past. Marcel, the narrator, is now, in the same sentence, musing with surprise over his having fallen asleep even though his mother never came in to say goodnight to him—he's in Combray, in the country house of his grandparents.

But, no, a new position in bed evokes a later memory, at Mme. de Saint-Loup's (who is she? how could we know?), where he's fallen into a drowsy sleep while he was supposed to be dressing for dinner. Now he reviews all the bedrooms of his entire life, a whole stream of bedrooms, and then—awake in present time again— he wills the evocation of memory, and we are again in Combray, with the narrator a child, a wildly sensitive child who is too preoccupied to sleep when he is sent off to bed. What he remembers first, in fact, is the "magic lantern" (a kind of early slide projector) given to him as a distraction for his sleepless bedroom; it sends revolving pictures of fairy tales onto the walls. "But I cannot express the uneasiness caused in me by this intrusion of mystery and beauty into a room I had at last filled with myself to the point of paying no more attention to the room than to that self. The anesthetizing influence of habit having ceased, I would begin to have thoughts, and feelings, and they are such sad things." And we are off again.

This is a novel rich in social detail, full of intrigue and event and passion both thwarted and satisfied, but its keenest interest is in what might be called the play of thought. It is much more than play for Proust; it is the essence of experience, the bedrock of everything, the ineffable underlayer of being human. No particulars (much as he loves the intricacy of the particular) are equal to the process of connection itself, and its hope of linking the smeared impermanence of events to the sublime of the eternal.

Proust's influence has been greater than even he (at once secretive, humble, and grandiose) could have guessed. Many generations of writers have been moved to emulate his exacting use of sensory detail, his obsessive examination of the self's responses to the world, and his emphasis on minute fluctuations of feeling. More lessons might be taken from his handling of time. His first and simplest message on the subject is that time in fiction is supremely flexible. A character turning over in bed *can* take thirty pages, why not? If interior life is going to be chronicled as closely as one of Mme. Verdurin's evening parties, a report of it can have the fluidity and expansiveness and sudden leaps across years that are the freedom of the noncorporeal. It should probably be said that this is not an unanchored freedom. The seven-volume work has a design, a construction with links—connection is its point. No commentary on the whole of *In Search of Lost Time* fails to cite its "architecture." That's the dazzling part. But a bold belief in flexibility is how the effect is achieved.

Everyone knows that a bad imitation of Proust is soporific and precious, which means that too much importance is placed on matters too trivial or feelings too slight to bear such close deliberation. Slowed time is—or should be—a way of pointing to what's important. This unveiling of importance is seen clearly in a very short piece by Kathy Boudin that I'm going to quote in full:

Water Rites

The key pushed into the lock, metal grating. The door opened.

Fifteen minutes, the gray-dressed man said, removing the barrier between the woman and the rest of the world.

She lived alone, behind a steel door with a slit of a window, twenty-three hours a day. Now she picked up her towel and soap dish and stepped outside the cell into a narrow corridor with seven other cells, four on each side. To someone who lived in a six by eight foot space, the small corridor felt as big as a yard.

She lifted each leg as it slowly moved past the other, feeling her leg muscles work as if they were rusty pedals on a bicycle. Two steps brought her alongside another window and, when a head appeared at the window, her lips said a silent "Hi" and turned at the corners into a smile.

But she had to keep walking, and two more steps brought her parallel to another window which did not have a face in it. Two more steps past a second empty window, two more until she arrived at a steel door with a handle. She reached for it, conscious of the power of being able to open a door herself. And pulled at it slowly, savoring the process.

Stepping inside the shower area, she pulled the door toward her, leaving a crack for air. Then she reached behind her with her right hand, pulling off the left sleeve of her robe, and then brought her left hand across her chest and pulled off her right sleeve. Dropping the robe on a wooden bench, she walked naked into another small room, one with a door that she could also open and close herself.

She ran her hands through her hair and took a deep breath: it came out slowly like a radiator releasing built-up steam.

Now she reached for the metal handle, trying to remember from the last time, and the time before and the time before that, the precise point to set it so that the perfect mix of warm and cold would come out. She turned it with her right hand, standing as far back as her arm allowed, and felt the spattering of cold as the handle passed through the cold range. Then the water grew warmer and she stopped turning, noting once again where that perfect spot was. She took a step toward the spray, bowing so that the full stream of it hit the top of her head and her shoulders and the first drops rolled down her back, which she arched, like a cat feeling a warm hand. Then she

lifted her face, letting the spray hit first her forehead,
then the nose and cheeks, the mouth and the chin
until her whole face felt it. In that moment she disappeared, as if this life had flowed off with the water.

This was written for a slow motion assignment in a
writing workshop at Bedford Hills Correctional Facility
given by the writer Hettie Jones. The suggestion was to
"see how slowed down you can get it."

I remembered this piece long after I first read it, and
it still seems a peerless illustration of how pacing points
to meaning. What might be regarded as the most mundane of activities—a shower—has a depiction that exactly conveys its importance. The intensity of sensory
detail mounts (as in Proust), step by step, particular by
particular, to a realm beyond itself, a vanishing point:
"in that moment she disappeared."

Fabulous Time

In talking about time, once we turn to nonrealistic fiction—all those stories with action beyond the possible, from magic realism all the way back to the folktale—it's clear that we need to ask different questions of this work. If we're in a realm where the laws of space and time need not operate according to the usual rules, how might a writer use that freedom, and what different techniques are needed?

We've been looking so far at ways of handling time with the assumption that we're meant to "believe" such events could have happened, that verisimilitude or mimesis is a needed component of the story. But in the long history of storytelling, realism is only one strain. For every closely observed *Moll Flanders* (1722) or *Clarissa* (1747–48), there's a wild and crazy *Tristram Shandy* (1759–67) or a fantastical *Gulliver's Travels* (1726). Even the most hardheaded of realists (I may be among their number) have been expanded and enlightened about fiction's possibilities from reading nonrealistic stories. The term *fabulous time* is an attempt to detail what's learned from this delight.

The convenient term *fabulation*—meaning story invention with an element of fantasy—is probably traceable to Robert Scholes's 1967 book, *The Fabulators,* a study of Durrell, Vonnegut, Southern, Hawkes, Murdoch, and Barth, writers then in the literary foreground. The term *magic realist* and the rich list of Latin American writers in its first generation—Rulfo, Carpentier, Fuentes, García Márquez—was just beginning its majestic surge. Writers from Gogol to Kafka to Borges and Nabokov were cited as predecessors. A count of more contemporary practitioners might include Salman Rushdie, Angela Carter, Jeanette Winterson, and Haruki Murakami (though not all of his works). In fact we are no longer so very picky or polemical about who's in what category, and writers move back and forth.

My ruminations on nonrealistic time really began in thinking about the famous first sentence of Gabriel García Márquez's *One Hundred Years of Solitude*: "Many years later, as he faced the firing squad, Colonel Aureliano Buendía was to remember that distant afternoon when his father took him to discover ice." In my experience, at any gathering of fiction writers—a party, a meal at an art colony, an academic meeting—more than one person can recite this first line by heart. One of its beauties is that it contains past, present, and future all in one sentence.

The future for Aureliano Buendía is the anticipated shot of the firing squad. The firing squad! Many pages later, we will in fact discover that this Aureliano Buendía doesn't die in these circumstances. But the sentence holds him in the moment of facing the rifles, and in what he thinks is his final instant he recalls an incident from childhood: "At that time Macondo was a village of twenty adobe houses. . . . The world was so recent that many things lacked names, and in order to indicate them it was necessary to point." That's a very *early* childhood—how could a man who lives to face the technology of rifles have grown up in such a world? He is from Macondo, town of the elemental, an eccentric spot in a teeming landscape whose inclusion of deeply varied pockets of history evokes a reality of Latin America, where isolated villages are embedded in the shadow of modern cities.

In Macondo, gypsies show up every March to display wonders—magnets, a telescope, a magnifying glass, an astrolabe, a compass. José Arcadio Buendía, father of the Aureliano in the first sentence, buys and experiments with all of them and befriends the aging gypsy Melquíades. Intoxicated with metaphysical speculation, José Arcadio thinks of setting out beyond Macondo, an expedition blocked by his wife. And then a new troupe of gypsies arrives, and their bazaar includes a tent in which a giant, guarding a pirate chest, lifts the lid to show "the overwhelming novelty of the sages of Memphis," advertised as having "belonged to King Solomon"—it's "an enormous, transparent block with infinite internal needles in which the light of the sunset was broken up into colored stars." José Arcadio tells his sons, "It's the largest diamond in the world," but the gypsy says no, it's ice. When Aureliano, a young boy, is allowed to touch it, he says, "It's boiling." His father, with his hand on the cake of ice, says, "This is the greatest invention of our time."

We are going to live through six more chapters of the family's complicated history before we reach the point "many years later" when Aureliano is before the firing squad. He is saved at the last second on page 141 of a 448-page book (a third of the way through). He will sire seventeen Aurelianos by his wife and one by a lover, and three generations after him another Aureliano will end the book, and the town of Macondo will reach its own exhaustion and finale.

As a reader can almost tell just from the first sentence, time in *One Hundred Years of Solitude* is both circular and linear. Repetition occurs lavishly and constantly, in a fecundity of recurrence and return. A family tree is supplied in the frontispiece, to provide a key to the repeating names: family members keep getting named Aureliano and Arcadio and José and Remedios and Úrsula and Amaranta, in changing combinations. Incidents recur, in varying forms: obsessions resprout, family failings reappear to cause new complications. The first José Arcadio Buendía cannot stop searching for the

Philosopher's Stone; a later Colonel Aureliano Buendía spends his old age making and unmaking little golden fish; and a yet later José Arcadio Segundo spends his last days studying the coded parchments of Melquíades's manuscripts. The red ants that keep invading the house come back again and again. Time passes as a series of cycles.

Richly crowded novels are not new—who could have more characters in one novel than Dickens?—but García Márquez is daring in his insistence that a fictional narrative can approach time by going around and around. The traditional visual metaphor for plot is a triangle, not a circle. Another brilliant novel by García Márquez is the shorter, more streamlined *Chronicle of a Death Foretold*, in which the call-and-response of what everybody knows and what finally happens forms a spiral of suspended expectation. A bride is returned to her family by her new husband because she is not a virgin. Beaten by her brothers, she is forced to reveal the name of her seducer. Everyone "knows" the bride's brothers will have to kill him. Does the doomed man know? Can he be warned? Can he somehow slip away? Did the bride lie? The town becomes a map of evaded encounters and random meetings, as chances keep crossing and doubling each other.

One Hundred Years of Solitude, with its luxuriant prolixities of repetition, forces the question: how can narrative drive be maintained if one is always turning back? It is worth looking at how García Márquez's techniques for handling time hold up the tumultuous mass of his book. It's clear enough that repetition is a way of anchoring an ornate narrative, of suggesting a grid of order within an overspill of invention. Readers trying to talk about the structure of *One Hundred Years of Solitude* find themselves saying, "Well, it's made up of a lot of separate stories." García Márquez gets us across a hundred years by amassing numerous separate chronicles. Repetition is how all these stories end up making sense together in one book.

One of García Márquez's other practices is the use of exaggerated image. His characters are obsessed with one thing—a notion or a principle or a person—that gets to work itself out fully in action. What does this have to do with handling time? The fixed ideas that take hold of his characters mean that readers don't have to spend pages hearing about everything else. We get to jump over intervening details and go right to the heart of the matter—exaggeration is a way to channel and focus the movement of time. This exaggeration is also characteristic of the much older form of the folktale, in which everything is kept simple and the plot hangs on a single line of action and result.

Like a folktale, *One Hundred Years of Solitude* is also told by an invisible all-seeing narrator. The voice who can tell us "Many years later, as he faced the firing squad, Colonel Aureliano Buendía was to remember that distant afternoon when his father took him to discover ice" is a witness at once sweeping and intimate. The teller's-eye view is from the cosmos and also from inside characters' heads. The narrator can cover everything for us, with all due speed and all due lingering.

García Márquez himself has said that he was heavily influenced by the tales told by his grandmother. If repetition, circularity, and exaggeration mark his use of time in an extremely complex novel, can a plain short tale illustrate these techniques as well? I'd like to look at a basic folktale in this light.

A handy example is the first tale in Italo Calvino's 1956 collection, *Italian Folktales.* The title of this tale has been translated into English as "Dauntless Little John" (it's *senza paura,* "without fear," in the Italian). John (Giovannin), wandering the world, is told there is no room at an inn, but he can stay at a haunted palace if he's willing. The palace is so notorious that friars automatically show up in the morning to carry away the dead body of anyone brave enough to stay, but John is game.

While he's sitting eating a sausage for supper in the palace, a voice calls out, "Shall I throw it down?" John says, "Go ahead!" and a man's leg falls down the chimney. The voice asks again, "Shall I throw it down?" John says throw and another leg, and then an arm, and then another arm arrive—and "then came the trunk of a body, and the arms and legs stuck onto it, and there stood a man without a head." At last a head is thrown down, and a giant hovers over Little John. The giant wants John to go with him. John says, "You lead the way." In this fashion, with John insisting that the giant precede him, they go down a stairway; John refuses to raise a stone slab and tells the giant to do it, and John, refusing again, gets the giant to carry three pots of gold up the stairs. The spell is then broken. The giant's arms, legs, head begin to disassemble, as the giant's voice calls out that a pot of gold is for John, a pot is for the friars, and the last pot is for the first poor man who comes by. And the giant's remains disappear up the chimney. John lives his life out as a wealthy man, in the once-haunted palazzo. "Then one day what should he do but look behind him and see his shadow: he was so frightened he died."

The story depends on repetitions that are close to chants. The giant's body parts arrive and leave in a list, and the giant's commands and John's countercommands form a similar chain. Reversal is the key to breaking the spell—the fierce giant obeys and does exactly what he's told John to do—and the plot leads to a reversal of fortune: a man with no place to stay winds up owning a palace. Exaggeration is, of course, the mode of the whole story: giants, flying heads, limbs that reattach, endless gold. Everything is bigger and more extreme than in what we think of as real life. A surprise reversal ends the story, a bit of comic irony in which a common trick of light scares the man without fear.

Repetition and reversal are not quite the same as a cycle—I don't want to overstretch the comparison to García Márquez—but general resemblances are evident. And the ending to this folktale is unmistakably circular. The man whose refusal to be afraid once broke a giant's spell is spooked to death by his own shadow—pulled down from his glory—and the story returns to the world where ordinary mortals are full of fear.

I began this chapter by saying that novelists of all stripes have learned from the time techniques employed in nonrealistic novels. Circularity as a key element of structure is beautifully evidenced in Arundhati Roy's *The God of Small Things*, first published in 1997—a novel set in the south Indian state of Kerala, a natural landscape presented with the sensory intensity of García Márquez's Macondo. ("It was raining when Rahel came back to Ayemenem. Slanting silver ropes slammed into loose earth, ploughing it up like gunfire. The old house on the hill wore its steep, gabled roof pulled over its ears like a low hat. . . . The wild, overgrown garden was full of the whisper and scurry of small lives. In the undergrowth a rat snake rubbed itself against a glistening stone.")

Rahel has returned to see her twin, Estha, a man she hasn't seen for many years. She and Estha are the age—thirty-one—that their mother was when she died. We hear about the twins' birth and then suddenly, on page 4, Rahel is remembering the funeral of her eight-year-old cousin, Sophie Mol, laid in "a special child-sized coffin." There is an unsettling visit to a police station after the funeral, and Estha (then seven) is shortly afterward sent to live with his father in Calcutta. He has just been sent home—"re-Returned"—by this father, all these years later.

The first chapter has portentous references to incidents no reader could yet identify. These references continue as the novel assumes its pattern of settling into one time frame (the arrival of Sophie Mol and her mother, Margaret, for instance) only to drift to another (early stages of the twins' mother's marriage). Each character's history is recounted and various side stories are filled in (how the grandmother and her maid became addicted to television, how the young Estha was molested at a cinema, how the History House once contained a pederast minister, how the twins' mother died alone in a grimy room in Aleppey, how Velutha the "untouchable" Paravan was the twins' favorite adult). Sophie Mol is mentioned and rementioned, and the reader keeps waiting for the circumstances of her death to be filled in at last.

The novel is circling Sophie Mol's death—spinning away from it, coming back, moving out again. Each time the death is mentioned, a little more information is fed to us, yet the scene directly depicting it remains out of reach. We keep expecting it soon, but, no. Only by gradual and seemingly disparate steps do we see how the loss of Sophie Mol is connected to a doomed love affair, to a ruthless political power play, to colonial effects on class aspiration, to the outrages of the caste system, to petty personal spite and monstrous pride, and to accident. In short: to all the other characters and their fates. Sophie Mol doesn't die onstage until page 293 of a 339-page book. By this time we know all the consequences of her death—the other deaths it causes, the lives it ruins—and the full nature of the tragedy. The details of the event come last.

It's not all that unusual for a book to begin with strong hints about the final outcome, to incite reader interest. What Arundhati Roy does here is much more intricately designed than that, a structure of repetition closer to the plan of a work like *One Hundred Years of Solitude.* In García Márquez's masterwork, a long drama of repetitions needs a century and multiple generations to play out its full scheme, the full span of its connected web. In Roy's book, no character's story can be narrated without catching on the hook of this one incident.

The repeated citing of Sophie Mol's death is what gives fire to the final drama. We have been waiting for how-it-happened for a long time, and Roy then has the burden of delivering it at last with sufficient power to reward our frustrations. Her success is the triumph of the method: our intense attachment to these characters, from knowing them so well before and *after* the event, makes the grief and violence of the last pieces of the puzzle count very heavily indeed.

Roy's decision to narrate her story in this way also allows her to render the language and impressions of a child without getting us stuck in a child's limits. We are with both the adult and the child. Most of the "magical" elements of the story are the child's interpretations: "Only Rahel noticed Sophie Mol's secret cartwheel in her coffin." This contact with a young consciousness is a key impulse behind the novel, so the mode serves the author's intentions wonderfully well. Most important of all, the circular pattern of telling makes the story feel fated, unfolding like a plot that can't be stopped. An Indian reviewer praised the novel as "an uncoiling spring of human foreboding and inevitability"—a lovely description of how the circular mode can have the vivid, highly colored certainty of a folktale or a legend.

Time as Subject

As I've thought about time in fiction for this essay, it's struck me that storytelling, in ancient and modern practice, is always a contemplation of the experience of time passing. A story depends on things not standing still, on the built-in condition of impermanence. All the emotions that attach to the passage of time—regret, impatience, anticipation, mourning, the longing for what's past, the desire for recurrence, the dread of recurrence—are the fuel of plots.

So by now it seems to me that narrative—because it shows events unfolding—always has time itself as an element of its subject matter. This can be seen more clearly as we turn to stories that do this quite directly, stories whose characters announce themselves as engaged in a particular struggle with time. There's the plot of remembering, in F. Scott Fitzgerald's "Winter Dreams," the plot of revised time, in Katherine Anne Porter's "Old Mortality," the plot of forgetting, in Denis Johnson's "Out on Bail," and the plot of unused time, in Henry James's "The Beast in the Jungle" and Leo Tolstoy's "The Death of Ivan Ilych." In thinking about the plots of these works, we will keep coming up against death's role in the very idea of story, mortality's natural link with closure.

This focus on content will also lead us to fiction that overtly declares the metaphysics of time to be its subject, with the example of Alan Lightman's *Einstein's Dreams.* And, after our long perusal of fiction with some degree of global reach, it seems right to close with a reminder of how culture regulates the marking of time, as seen in Chinua Achebe's *Things Fall Apart.*

Stories of "never forgetting" are perhaps the widest category of all, since much fiction depends on characters who refuse to, in our modern parlance, get over it. I am thinking of the elderly lovers in García Márquez's *Love in the Time of Cholera,* who wait a lifetime for consummation; or the Irish soldier in Frank O'Connor's "Guests of the Nation," who obeys the order to execute an English prisoner he's come to know well and is left to conclude, in one of fiction's great closing lines: "And anything that ever happened to me after I never felt the same about again." Not letting go is often the honor of such characters, as well as the spine of the action or the spirit of the outcome.

A milder, more melancholic form of this stubborn remembrance infuses Fitzgerald's "Winter Dreams." It begins with the young Dexter Green, "not more than fourteen," quitting his job as a caddie at a golf club in Minnesota. Dexter has quit due to the "emotional shock" of being called "boy" and issued commands by a pretty, spoilt little girl named Judy Jones. "Several years later,"

Dexter has achieved great business success, and on the golf course he again meets Judy Jones, who's now "arrestingly beautiful." He is lying on a raft after a nighttime swim when she comes by in a motorboat, and their romance begins. Once she's invited him for dinner at her house and they're kissing, "it did not take him many hours to decide that he had wanted Judy Jones ever since he was a proud, desirous little boy."

Judy is exhilarating, seductive, headstrong, fickle— her "exquisite excitability" moves her from one romantic adventure to the next. She is always drawing Dexter in and sending him away and drawing him back. He finally gives up and becomes engaged to another girl, "light-haired and sweet and honorable, and a little stout." He is settling into this nicely when he sees Judy at a dance. Judy manages to get him alone and say, "Oh, Dexter, have you forgotten last year?" He allows as he has not, and step by step—with tears and vows— she lures him back. Their rekindled romance, causing much pain around them, lasts no more than a month, and soon after he goes off to war.

Seven years later, more successful than ever, he is chatting with a business acquaintance who tells him that the wife of one of his best friends happens to be from Dexter's hometown:

> "Judy Jones she was once. . . . I'm sort of sorry for
> her. . . . [Her husband] has gone to pieces in a way.

I don't mean he ill-uses her, but he drinks and runs around. . . . She's a little too old for him," said Devlin.

"Too old!" cried Dexter. "Why, man, she's only twenty-seven!"

Dexter cannot hear the report without incredulous indignation. When the man says, "She was a pretty girl when she first came to Detroit," Dexter shouts that "she wasn't a pretty girl, at all," she was a "great beauty," and the man can only say, "Lots of women fade just like *that*. . . . She has nice eyes."

Dexter is stunned. "He had thought that having nothing else to lose he was invulnerable at last—but he knew that he had lost something more, as surely as if he had married Judy Jones and seen her fade away before his eyes." He conjures up his memories of summer nights and moonlit verandas and "the gold color of her neck's soft down. . . . Why, these things were no longer in the world! They had existed and they existed no longer."

Time's passage is fresh news to Dexter. He can't quite get his mind around this plainest of truths. And it's the job of art to make old human facts new. (No writer could put this more eloquently than James Baldwin, in "Sonny's Blues," when Sonny's music is finally heard in the last scene: "while the tale of how we suffer, and how we are delighted, and how may triumph is never new, it always must be heard. There isn't any other tale to tell, it's the only light we've got in all this darkness.") Dexter, shocked to the core, joins all those who have contemplated the snows of yesteryear. Fitzgerald, as a writer, is especially in love with youth and beauty and glamour and always takes their vanishing very hard. And Dexter has no shame in assuming the woe in this is, as we would say, all about him: "long ago, there was something in me, but now that thing is gone."

The Japanese have the term *mono no aware,* used to indicate an awareness of the transience of life (literally "the pathos of things"). It is an aesthetic emotion and a highly valued one. Impermanence is built into all experience, and the reminder of this has its own exquisite poignancy. The cherry blossoms that bloom and fall within a week are Japan's yearly celebration of this apprehension of beauty.

Fitzgerald is hardly a Buddhist in his thinking—acceptance is not where he or his heroes rest. "Winter Dreams" was published in 1922, when Fitzgerald could not have been more than twenty-six, and the passage of youth struck him as particularly unbearable. While the reader's experience of "Winter Dreams" is not necessarily the same as Dexter's—those are his tears, not ours—the sequence of the narrative does evoke Judy's bloom into beauty. We meet her before her blossoming and we hear of her after. It is the afterward that wounds the glory in Dexter's memory. Simple as this story is, it carries forth an ancient theme of fiction, the dilemma of transience.

The fog of *other* people's remembering is the theme of Katherine Anne Porter's "Old Mortality" (1937), in which a family clings to its legend of beautiful, reckless Amy, who died young. She is Aunt Amy, their father's lost sister, to Maria and Miranda, age twelve and eight at the story's opening, whose dual point of view filters the key actions through most of the piece. The girls have "always" been told that the impeccably glamorous Amy threw herself away by marrying her devoted cousin Gabriel, whom she didn't love, and neglected her delicate health, on purpose, and died soon after. Gabriel, long remarried, still buys a wreath for Amy's grave every year. The most amazing detail to the girls is that their "pleasant, everyday" father once shot at a man who was seen kissing Amy when he was not engaged to her.

The layers of information recall Alice Munro's later methods in stories like "The Progress of Love." Events are seen one way at first, and then seen through other lenses. In the first section of "Old Mortality," we hear what seem to be direct quotes—Amy is cynical, wickedly amused, despairing—and we hear comments a generation later from adoring relatives, reminiscing. The sisters, after they're "grown," discover a blithely brittle letter, written by Amy on her honeymoon, and another from a nurse explaining an allegedly accidental overdose.

Part II has Maria and Miranda, now fourteen and ten, schoolgirls in a New Orleans convent, taken out to the races to watch their uncle Gabriel's horse run. Gabriel is a "shabby fat man with bloodshot blue eyes, sad beaten eyes, and a big melancholy laugh, like a groan"—not at all the "handsome romantic beau" of family legend. To everyone's surprise, Gabriel's horse wins. Miranda is horrified when she later sees the horse bleeding from the nostrils and is also sure her uncle is "a drunkard." The girls are taken to a cheap hotel for a disastrous meeting with their uncle's "gloomy" and profoundly bitter second wife, Miss Honey.

In Part III, the point of view is solely Miranda's, and she is a young woman, "just past eighteen," on a train. She is seated next to a bucktoothed, chinless, "ferocious" old lady, who turns out to be Cousin Eva, homely since youth, unmarried, a teacher of Latin. They are both going home for Gabriel's funeral.

Eva has an alternate version of the Amy legend. She insists, against Miranda's objections, that Amy once tried to run off to elope with the man Miranda's father shot at. She says it did look odd that Amy rose from a sickbed to suddenly marry Gabriel, and her death six weeks later had "something very mysterious" about it. Eva, who's been jailed in campaigns for women's right to vote, tells Miranda, "You mustn't live in a romantic haze about life." But Miranda has already been married a year, a "situation" for which she now feels only "an immense weariness." Not only does Eva suggest that Amy was pregnant and killed herself from fear of disgrace, but Eva says she never found her that beautiful either. Her flushed complexion was from tuberculosis, which she brought on "by drinking lemon and salt to stop her periods when she wanted to go to dances. . . . They fancied that young men could tell what ailed them by touching their hands, or even by looking at them. . . . You can't imagine what the rivalry was like. . . . It was just sex. Their minds dwelt on nothing else."

Miranda thinks that Eva's scornful version is "no more true" than what she's been told and "every bit as romantic." When they arrive home, and Eva is suddenly in lively, happy conversation with Miranda's father, Miranda is glad not to be able to overhear their familiar stories. "Old Mortality" closes with her repudiating vow: "At least I can know the truth about what happens to me, she assured herself silently, making a promise to herself, in her hopefulness, her ignorance."

Katherine Anne Porter is as enchanted by glamour as Fitzgerald is, as spiritually tuned to the "gorgeous" (to use a term Fitzgerald uses fondly in "Absolution"). She mocks the militant dowdiness of Cousin Eva and even has her mourn a blue velvet gown she once had. But the movement of "Old Mortality" is to resolutely keep cutting away the false beauty of the past, layer by layer.

The girls' first version of Amy is that she's sweetly dead, quaint, and overdiscussed. Even as she emerges as more vital and scandalous, the adults insist that her high spirits made her all the more lovable. The passages in which she is quoted begin to sound more bitingly fatalistic (we are looking over Miranda's and Maria's shoulders, seeing more than they can), and the suggested suicide is not a surprise. But it's the shabby alcoholism of Gabriel and the inelegant depression of his wife that debunk the romance for Miranda. She needs her own treat of a day at the races gone sour to teach her about rosy notions lost.

And the glory of horse racing is broken forever when Miranda sees the horse's suffering and blood. Physicality is much of what's been left out of family memories. Eva supplies this—citing pregnancy, menstruation, and the symptoms of disease. And could tuberculosis really be "brought on" by drinking lemon and salt? I read this as Eva's own invention, a fitting end to a story of continuing corrections.

The story can be seen as deconstructing most of the models (some of them particularly Southern) that Miranda and Maria are raised to revere, including the power of the Belle, gambling as a gentleman's pastime, and romantic ruin. In the end, femaleness itself is de-idealized.

These illusions come to Miranda from a family in love with remembering. Aunt Amy, a vivid presence throughout the sisters' growing up, is not someone they've ever met. Most of the action is rendered as-told-to (only the second section at the race is all in current time); incidents are spoken of so often they feel like experiences to Maria and Miranda. Even as children they think of themselves as containing other people's memories.

We are in the girls' heads but we also hear the writer commenting on them (limited omniscience), and Porter is especially supple in using this mode in the story's final passages. Miranda, who's had more than enough of her family's insistence on sentimentalizing the past, feels sure that she can at least see what's going on in her own life, but the author (who lives somewhere in the future) is aware of how young Miranda is. Miranda's resolve to live without distortions is happening in a period that will seem different later, when the movement of years takes her past this moment of "her hopefulness, her ignorance."

If memory is essential to fiction, what of writers whose characters insist on remembering as little as they can? Denis Johnson's "Out on Bail," from his 1992 collection

Jesus' Son, is a model narrative of forgetting. It begins, "I saw Jack Hotel in an olive-green three-piece suit, with his blond hair combed back and his face shining and suffering." People are buying Jack drinks because he's being tried for armed robbery and is on lunch break from the courthouse. Somehow Jack has kept this a secret till now. It looks bad for Jack—twenty-five years minimum. Jack is maybe nineteen.

The narrator looks around the bar—"a long, narrow place, like a train car that wasn't going anywhere"—filled with people who "all seemed to have escaped from someplace." About his alleged crime, Jack can only say, "It happened a long time ago. . . . It was last year."

The worst things in the narrator's life have happened in this bar, but he keeps coming back here, looking for love. "And then I would remember I had a wife at home who loved me, or later that my wife had left me and I was terrified, or again later that I had a beautiful alcoholic girlfriend who would make me happy forever."

He sits that night in a booth with Kit Williams, a boxer who's in his fifties: "He'd wasted his entire life. Such people were very dear to those of us who'd wasted only a few years." The narrator suddenly remembers that, actually, he heard weeks ago that Jack Hotel was going to trial, and he suddenly realizes that the celebration at lunch was over Hotel's acquittal. "There were many moments in the Vine like that one—where you might think today was yesterday, and yesterday was tomorrow, and so on. Because we all believed we were tragic, and we drank."

Bitter over Jack's acquittal, the police have told him to get out of town. He finally leaves after fighting with his girlfriend. He gets jobs further west, but washes up in town again a year later. The narrator, roaming the streets one night after a quarrel with his own girlfriend, runs into Jack when the bars open the next morning. "Sometimes what I wouldn't give to have us sitting in a bar again at 9:00 a.m. telling lies to one another, far from God."

The narrator invites Jack to join him while he steals a dead tenant's Social Security check and buys some heroin with it. He and Jack both go looking for their girlfriends, with the prize of drugs in hand. The narrator passes out—and when he comes to, his girlfriend and a neighbor are hovering over him: "I was overjoyed not to be dead." And Jack, who can't find his lover, does his share of the drugs and also passes out, in a rooming house. His friends there make sure the mist of his breath shows against a mirror:

> But after a while they forgot about him, and his breath failed without anybody's noticing. He simply went under. He died.
>   I am still alive.

No characters could have faultier memories than the ones who populate this story—not only have they lost track of all the days before, they can barely pay attention to the moment they're in. Forgetting makes things happen in this world, and the failure of attention, the lack of interest in consequences, does not have a good end. The narrator knows he is lucky not to be as dead as Jack. And yet he is fond of that bar, those times. The one flash-forward is a wry wish to have it all back. This loyalty to those days is the storyteller's impetus for the story, with its urge to explain, its asides, and its evocations of internal logic.

This is a fiction of consciousness, though it has absolutely none of the obsessively close detail, the attenuated cerebrations, that this term points to in Proust or Woolf. Johnson, in this story, wants to especially mention (*emphasize* may be too strong a term for a story that aims to be ambling) the slippage in the sensation of time. What day is it? Is he married to someone? Did he hear that before or later? To understand what has happened, we have to be led into a realm where losing track is ordinary—not hard to do at all—between tighter, brighter spots.

Johnson saves his most intense effect for the ending, and the reader may well be as surprised as the characters by Hotel's death. We didn't quite know we were in that sort of story. In fact, another author might have made the overdose the center of the story, its reason for being. But Johnson has orchestrated the sequence differently. We meet Jack at a much earlier phase and our first surprise is the sudden relief that he's not going to prison. Good news! Saved from twenty-five years! (This insistence on a "before" actually bears some resemblance to Fitzgerald's strategy of introducing Judy Jones as a child.) It's a great irony that his rescue does not last so very long after all.

The title, "Out on Bail," has meanings that shift as the story shifts. It would seem to refer to Jack Hotel—but, no, he's already freed when we meet him. It might point to how short Jack's time out of jail really turns out to be. And, at last look, it reminds us of the narrator's lucky reprieve from a sentence of death.

The story's strongest emotion is the stab of irony in Jack's unexpected exit from the stage. If time catches up with these people, one of Johnson's achievements in *Jesus' Son* is not to make any of it a moral lesson. He doesn't exactly care who pays for what sins. The point is elsewhere. It is embedded in the asides. If no one in the stories can remember much, almost every story in the collection contains a remark from the storyteller alluding to his being "still alive" in a later existence: "Sometimes what I wouldn't give to have us sitting in a bar again." Or (the first line of "The Other Man"), "But I never finished telling you about the two men." And most forcefully in "Emergency": "That world! These days it's all been erased and they've rolled it up like a scroll and put it away somewhere. Yes, I can touch it with my fingers. But where is it?"

The lost habits of forgetting are what the teller has the work of trying to remember. Where does the time *go?*

Another form of vanishing is seen in Henry James's classic story "The Beast in the Jungle" (1903). Any number of James's stories show us protagonists seeing that the chance to live fully has slipped away—they've waited for the wrong possibility, misunderstood what's been offered, chosen a deceptive promise, sacrificed themselves to no point. James is the great artist of the missed boat. In *The Ambassadors,* written just before "The Beast in the Jungle," his fiftyish protagonist pleads with a younger character, "Live all you can—it's a mistake not to. It doesn't so much matter what you do in particular, so long as you have your life. If you haven't had that, what have you had?"

In "The Beast in the Jungle," John Marcher, meeting May Bartram again after ten years, has to be reminded that he once told her a great secret: he's always believed that he's "being kept for something rare and strange, possibly prodigious and terrible." It won't be an achievement, it will be an experience—and it won't be falling in love, which has already happened and not been overwhelming. May, supremely sympathetic and understanding, agrees to "watch with" him for it.

She is already thirty, and their friendship continues for years, shaped by her constant discreet interest and marked by subtle references to the tremendous and perhaps fearful fate that lies in wait, the Beast in the Jungle. Marcher feels that his destiny cannot allow him to honorably marry anyone, and May is loyal to the particular form of friendship they have—"the odd irregular rhythm of their intensities and avoidances."

He occasionally notices that May is looking older. When he visits her in their mutual old age, he's convinced she knows something he doesn't. She does tell him that he won't "consciously suffer," and that his idea of something in wait is not wrong or past happening— "the door isn't shut." He expects her to tell more, but instead she closes her eyes, gives way "to a slow fine shudder," and says she is too ill to continue. "Too ill to tell me?" he says. He's afraid she'll die without telling, and she manages to say, "Don't you know—now?" She is fading, though she denies being in pain, and when he asks what has happened, she says, "What *was* to."

In later days, when May is too ill to see him, Marcher thinks she must have meant that her death—his solitude when he is no longer attended by her—will be the Beast he's waited for. But she recovers in time to tell him that the thing that was to come *has* come, and his not being aware is "the strangeness *in* the strangeness . . . the wonder of the wonder." Her last words to him are "I would live for you still—if I could. . . . But I can't!"

At her graveside, Marcher is dismayed at how private and unrecognized their lifelong connection is. And he feels not only robbed of her company but also cheated now of the constant sense of his great, lurking fate. It has passed and she has told him not to guess what it was. "The torment of this vision became then his occupation." He keeps trying to sort through "the lost stuff of consciousness" to find what she saw and he didn't. He ends by kneeling at her grave: "her two names became a pair of eyes that didn't know him. He gave them a last long look, but no palest light broke."

This is a long story (fifty-four pages in my compact paperback of James's short fiction), and its five sections are meant to evoke districts of long years passing. Marcher's obtuseness about May's great love for him—his missed chance—is a failure of imagination, egotism as a specialized misconcentration. Waiting to experience life more deeply than most people, he pretty much experiences nothing. Our sympathy is, of course, with May—it's her tragedy. One of James's nice ironies is that he shows her to us through Marcher's eyes and Marcher thinks she's splendid, which, oddly enough, is convincing to us too.

Most of the action in the story is internal. James's long

sentences trace the streams of qualified reasoning, the scruples and counterscruples, the intentions and corrections. Marcher has lived too stubbornly in his head and relied too much on futurity, like a scion waiting to come into an inheritance. James's famous advice to writers— "Try to be one of the people on whom nothing is lost"— is exemplified in reverse by Marcher.

But in a final coda, a section after the major action of the story seems to be over, Marcher visits May's grave again. A year has passed. At the cemetery, he sees a fellow mourner—"one of the deeply stricken"—and the "deep ravage" of his features causes Marcher to understand that he himself has "utterly, insanely missed" being touched by any comparable "passion": "He had seen *outside* of his life, not learned within it. . . . *She* was what he had missed." He sees what May saw: "The escape would have been to love her; then, *then* he would have lived. *She* had lived . . . whereas he had never thought of her . . . but in the chill of his egotism and the light of her use." The horror of this gives him, at last, a pain whose depth is precious—"that at least, belated and bitter, had something of the taste of life." But the horror undoes him; the beast of his fate has sprung.

Quite a lot of fiction looks at wasted, ruined, and unled lives (often more intriguing than well-led ones), but what is especially striking in this story is that it holds up to the light the entire question of what "wasted time" is. What Marcher has missed, in the end, is an essential privilege of being human, not only the experience of love but the will to imagine another consciousness.

"Lost time" has another definition in Leo Tolstoy's majestic story "The Death of Ivan Ilych" (1886). The story opens in a law court chamber. The lawyers read in the paper that Ivan Ilych, a colleague who was ill, has just died. Each is thinking, "Well, he's dead but I'm alive!" One lawyer makes a mourning call on the wife, who complains of the toll taken on her nerves by her husband's suffering and asks about a higher pension. The lawyer is glad to leave in time to get to his usual game of cards. These charades of helpless affectation and elemental dread are preamble to an account of the dead man.

"Ivan Ilych's life had been most simple and most ordinary and therefore most terrible." He is, from youth, "intelligent, polished, lively and agreeable" and all goes well for him, according to conventional notions of well. He sows a few wild oats when he's young, then settles into a pleasant enough marriage. But his wife soon becomes jealous and demanding, and Ivan Ilych, in his attempts to escape, devotes himself to his work. He lives in a marriage of "veiled hostility" alternating with occasional "islets" of "amorousness" and learns to regard this arrangement as entirely normal.

When he's passed over for a promotion at work, he becomes depressed and vindictive, but a change of fortune and a salary increase make him happy and likable again. He enchants himself buying new furnishings for their tasteful new home. He is on a stepladder showing how he wants the draperies to hang when he falls and injures himself.

He begins to have chronic pain and weakness. Self-important doctors give advice, but the pain worsens. When a relative visits and is plainly shocked by his appearance, Ilych realizes how ill he is. A new doctor has a new theory, but Ilych lies in bed and is terrified to think of dying. "I was here and now I'm going there! Where?"

His next stage is "continual despair"—"face to face with *It*. And nothing could be done with *It* except to look at it and shudder." The false comfort that surrounds him—the pretense that he will be well again—fills him with hate. In the third month of his illness, when he sees how the agony and mess of his decline are a trial to his household, he comes under the gentle care of the servant Gerasim. Ilych fancies that his pain ceases when his legs are held aloft on Gerasim's shoulders, and Gerasim alone is frank enough to say, "We shall all of us die, so why should I grudge a little trouble?"

It's all too clear to Ilych that the assumptions he's been running on all these years have no grounding, that what is before him now requires something quite other. He looks back on his life, and all except childhood seems tainted with falsity. How could that be? he thinks. His last three days are spent screaming in pain, but at the very last he has a sense of falling through a hole that has light at the bottom. His small son kisses his hand, and Ilych feels sorry for the son, and suddenly sorry too for his poor, shallow wife. He is able to tell them to take his son away, to spare him, and he tries to say "forgive me" but says "forego" instead:

> knowing that He whose understanding mattered would understand.
>   And suddenly it grew clear to him that what had been oppressing him and would not leave him was all dropping away at once.

He has a flood of great, abiding pity for all those around him, and he finds that his own pain is still there but no longer matters:

> In place of death there was light. . . .
>   To him all this happened in a single instant, and the meaning of that instant did not change. For those present his agony continued for another two hours.

When, at the very end, he hears someone say, "It is finished!" he can only think, "Death is finished. . . . It is no more!"

Tolstoy's boldness is to suggest that far more is required of people than they usually think. If Henry James's Marcher misses out because he believes in his own specialness, Ilych is always aware that he's a man like other men, no better and no worse. Losing, bit by bit, all that he's relied on forces him to see what no one else around him will. Once he comes out of himself enough to be overwhelmed by sorrow for the other humans nearby, he takes a further leap out of the self toward the divine.

It is plain what "wasted time" is in this story—it's a life of evasion, marked by scrambling toward false goals. Only Gerasim seems to have no trouble believing that death is a universal fate, and he has a different sort of ego and a different sense of how to spend time as a result of this understanding. Ilych, who attains clarity at the last, is like the grandmother described by the Misfit in Flannery O'Connor's "A Good Man Is Hard to Find": "She would of been a good woman . . . if it had been somebody there to shoot her every minute of her life." Ilych's illusions and his suffering fall away from him very late. But not too late.

"All stories, if continued far enough, end in death, and he is no true storyteller who would keep that from you." This is Hemingway's great sentence in *Death in the Afternoon,* a book not about fiction but about bullfighting. Formally speaking, it might be said all endings have as their models the final cut—the limit of all action. The mystery of what Buddhists call transience is embedded in every narrative. Even the lightest fiction, caught up in glamour or bloody adventure, knows that time's winged chariot is hurrying near and that our days are numbered.

There is a small but distinct tradition of fiction that is designed with the overt intention of dealing with time. Contemporary examples include Martin Amis's *Time's Arrow* (1991), in which time moves backward, and Charles Baxter's *First Light* (1987), in which each chapter is set at an earlier point than the previous one. We might look further back in the twentieth century to include Jorge Luís Borges's "The Secret Miracle" (1944), which posits a year of frozen time elapsing before a firing squad as a man composes his masterpiece, or its predecessor, Ambrose Bierce's "An Occurrence at Owl Creek Bridge" (1891), in which a man who is about to be hanged escapes and travels far, only to return to the moment of hanging.

Perhaps the most direct treatment of time as subject is Alan Lightman's *Einstein's Dreams* (1993), whose premise is that the young Einstein has been dreaming of alternate worlds with different kinds of time. One such world has been selected for his theory (the most "compelling" sort of time, presumably ours), but the others—equally "possible"—form the chapters of this book. One dream world has people repeating actions endlessly, not knowing they repeat; only those dogged by regret have the sleepless sense of an endless loop. In another world, travelers from the future try hard to be invisible, desperate not to interrupt the fate of unfolding events.

This is a fiction without named characters, but peopled by flat figures who live, like Einstein and his family, in Berne, Switzerland, in 1905. Some chapters mimic folktales. In the land where people live in the mountains to retain youth, the highlanders start valuing their thin air so much that they eat only "gossamer food" and thus age prematurely. Many of the chapters might be called philosophical fables. In the town where people are stuck in particular moments in time, it doesn't matter whether these are moments of pain or joy, because to be stuck is to be alone. And (another chapter tells us) in the center of time, there is no motion—is that contentment or lifelessness?

Like Italo Calvino's *Invisible Cities* (1972), the book moves in a shimmering serial progress of lyrically composed units ("poetic vignettes" is the phrase on the back of my paperback). There are periodic "interludes"—not dreams—in which Einstein in daylight speaks with his friend Besso. In the best of these, Einstein says he wants to understand time in order to "get close to The Old One," but Besso isn't sure The Old One has any interest in getting close to his creations, and is surprised Einstein wants to be close to anyone.

As readers, we are dazzled by the parade of permutations (a lifetime is one day long in one place, and in another it lasts forever) and their whimsically imagined consequences. What keeps recurring is the human desire to stop time, a longing always bound to be self-defeating. In the last dream, the city's entire population runs to catch birds in a flock—this flock of nightingales is time—"these birds are rarely caught." But every so often, a precious nightingale is exquisitely trapped in a jar, only to expire, since stillness and stoppage mean being "without life."

An epilogue has Einstein giving his manuscript about time to the typist, feeling only "empty" after the soaring of his thought. Lightman's book is also a kind of soaring headiness, a meditation on the dilemma of time as it's experienced and as it can be approached through metaphor. Lightman uses the methods of a cerebral Scheherazade—night after night of separate tales—to sound once more the plaint of time passing.

What I've written here has had the premise that people throughout the world necessarily have to deal with time as an element of their lives as self-conscious humans. But different cultures mark time differently. The variations that Alan Lightman posits through the landscape of dreams also arise in actual geography. No book could argue this more indelibly than Chinua Achebe's *Things Fall Apart* (1958), a novel that looks at the conflict between two different cultures' notions of time. It takes place in what is now Nigeria and chronicles the drama of one man's life within Ibo traditions of clan and caste and conduct, before contact with Europeans and after Christian missionaries arrive from England. The opening sentences set out its hero: "Okonkwo was well known throughout the nine villages and even beyond. His fame rested on solid personal achievements." His achievements include physical tenacity (he wins a match with a renowned wrestler), courage (at feasts he drinks from the skull of the first man he killed in battle), and resilience in the face of obstacles (born to no wealth, he successfully cultivates rich fields). His own father was a pleasure-loving ne'er-do-well and he is ever eager to escape this disgrace. This makes him hard on his own son, whose gentleness he tries to quash. The psychology of this family drama seems familiar and modern, and, in fact, much of the book's initial pleasures have to do with a sense of how much is recognizable within the (to us) exotic contours of the story.

Time for Okonkwo is regulated by the seasons of agriculture, and by traditions linked to them. Early on, he is penalized for beating one of his wives during the

Week of Peace; he has to bring sacrifices to a shrine, so crops aren't hurt by this transgression. Private conduct affects cosmic processes.

Laws regulate everything, but interpretation is crucial. Okonkwo's fatal flaw is his fear of being weak like his father. When the headman decrees that a boy who's lived with Okonkwo has to be killed, Okonkwo, eager to show his lack of sentiment, is overzealous in joining the ritual killing. His own son, horrified, is afraid of Okonkwo forever after.

In event after event, we see Okonkwo as a hot-tempered man constrained by a net of laws to be patient. Midway through the novel, a disaster happens at a funeral: Okonkwo's gun goes off by accident, killing a young man, and because "it was a crime against the earth goddess to kill a clansman," he is forced to go into exile to another village for seven years. During these years, while Okonkwo is waiting, missionaries begin to appear in the region. One of their early converts is Okonkwo's own alienated son, Nwoye, whose conversion is an incomprehensible anguish to Okonkwo.

Once he's back in his own village, the community cleverly invites the missionaries to build their church in the Evil Forest, a place of danger, but to its astonishment and dismay the church prospers. Nothing is holding together. When the annual worship of the earth goddess is violently disrupted by a convert, the clan rises up at last and destroys the church. Okonkwo is jubilant. The manly virtues he has spent a lifetime cultivating are called into service once again. And then he is thrown into the district prison, where he is beaten and humiliated. Upon his release to a much changed village—"All our gods are weeping"—an enraged Okonkwo uses his machete to kill a government messenger. He knows what his fate now is, and when the district commissioner comes for him, Okonkwo has eluded him by hanging himself, a death without honor.

One of the novel's great points is that the conflict between colonial and conquered is not merely about power; it's about opposing notions of natural order and the requirements of cyclical time. To the English Christians, seasonal heat and rain are matters of passing inconvenience. To the Ibo, these turns of weather not only are crucial to the crops but also are events that always require ritual anticipation and response. If traditional observance is broken, fatal effects erupt. Okonkwo's willed death is especially tragic because it violates the way things need to be: "It is an offense against the Earth, and a man who commits it will not be buried by his clansmen." Before the white officials, Okonkwo's best friend bursts into furious speech that "one of the greatest men" in the region has been driven to such a death.

From the novel's standpoint, this death is dramatically right—it provides a finish to the story on a tragic scale, and it gives us the shape of a hero's fate, from young manhood to death. Okonkwo's adult life span is the measure of the story's duration, as in the chronicle novels we considered earlier.

Things Fall Apart has a coda of sorts in the final paragraph, where the point of view shifts to the district commissioner, who enjoys thinking that he might write a book about all he's learned in Africa: "One could almost write a whole chapter on [Okonkwo]. Perhaps not a whole chapter but a reasonable paragraph, at any rate." We're left with a double irony of scale—the reduction of the great Okonkwo to a brief passage in an unwritten book, and the reduction of the commissioner to a paragraph in this great novel.

It strikes me again how many works of fiction end with a character's death, from Flaubert to Achebe. The use and reuse of death as an ending points to the inevitable resemblance between the arc of story and the arc of an individual existence rising and falling. It indicates, among other things, how elemental form is, and the profound instincts that underlie a tale teller's efforts to bring a story to a close.

"All stories, if continued far enough, end in death." The sequence of any fiction is, by its nature, the path of time evaporating. I began by talking about duration, how much time a story decides to cover, where it draws its borders. Once, many years ago, I was sent to talk to third graders in a public school in New York, a noisy school with security guards in the hall and good teachers. The directive was to read from a book I'd especially liked as a child and then to talk about being a writer. Afterward, one kid wanted to know about the lady who wrote the story I'd read (a World War II saga)—was she still alive? And another kid wanted to know about this book of my own I'd held up—was it hard to get the covers on? I thought both questions were about the mystery of containment. How is the book held together, how is it here if the writer isn't, how does the story stay still?

I might have cited Shakespeare—they were too young for Shakespeare—but Sonnet 19 would have answered them, with its insistence on verse living on ever young, despite Devouring Time. The kids in that auditorium are in their late twenties now, probably a bit surprised themselves they got to be so old, a surprise every real story is onto.

Works Discussed

Achebe, Chinua. *Things Fall Apart.*

Bennett, Arnold. *The Old Wives' Tale.*

Boudin, Katherine. "Water Rites," in *More In Than Out,* ed. Hettie Jones.

Carver, Raymond. "Chef's House," in *Cathedral.*

Chekhov, Anton. "The Darling," in *Anton Chekhov's Short Stories,* ed. Ralph E. Matlaw.

Connell, Evan S. *Mrs. Bridge.*

DeLillo, Don. "Videotape," in *Sudden Fiction (Continued),* ed. Robert Shapard and James Thomas.

Fitzgerald, F. Scott. *The Great Gatsby.*

Fitzgerald, F. Scott. "Winter Dreams," in *All the Sad Young Men.*

Flaubert, Gustav. "A Simple Heart," in *Three Tales,* trans. Robert Baldick.

Forster, E. M. *Aspects of the Novel.*

García Márquez, Gabriel. *Chronicle of a Death Foretold,* trans. Gregory Rabassa.

García Márquez, Gabriel. *One Hundred Years of Solitude,* trans. Gregory Rabassa.

Italian Folktales, selected and retold by Italo Calvino, trans. George Martin.

James, Henry. "The Beast in the Jungle."

Johnson, Denis. "Out on Bail," in *Jesus' Son.*

Kierkegaard, Søren. *The Diary of Søren Kierkegaard.*

Lightman, Alan. *Einstein's Dreams.*

Maupassant, Guy de. *A Woman's Life,* trans. H. N. P. Sloman.

Munro, Alice. "Differently," "The Progress of Love," "Carried Away," "The Albanian Virgin," in *Selected Stories.*

Poe, Edgar Allan. "The Importance of the Single Effect in a Prose Tale," in *The Story and Its Writer,* sixth edition, ed. Ann Charters.

Porter, Katherine Anne. "Old Mortality," in *Pale Horse, Pale Rider.*

Proust, Marcel. *In Search of Lost Time,* trans. Lydia Davis.

Roy, Arundhati. *The God of Small Things.*

Steegmuller, Francis. "Ciao Fabrizio," in *When in Rome,* ed. Robert Wechsler.

Stendhal. *The Red and the Black,* trans. Lowell Bair.

Tolstoy, Leo. "The Death of Ivan Ilych," trans. Louise and Aylmer Maude.

Woolf, Virginia. *To the Lighthouse.*

Woolf, Virginia. *A Writer's Diary.*

Yu Hua. *To Live,* trans. Michael Berry.

Acknowledgments

"Long Time" first appeared, in slightly altered form, as part of "Long Times in Short Stories, or Why Can't a Story Be More Like a Novel?" in the *Writer's Chronicle,* February 2004.

"Water Rites," by Kathy Boudin, from *More In Than Out,* edited by Hettie Jones (published by the Writing Workshop at Bedford Hills Correctional Facility) is reprinted by special permission of the author.

Special thanks to Kathleen Hill for the wisdom of her insights and the generosity of her conversation. And I am thankful, now and always, to Carol Houck Smith, who first suggested I write about time in an essay. How we miss you, dear Carol.

JOAN SILBER is the author of six books of fiction, including *The Size of the World* and *Ideas of Heaven*, which was a finalist for the National Book Award and the Story Prize. In 2007 Silber received a Literature Award from the American Academy of Arts and Letters. She teaches at Sarah Lawrence College and lives in New York City.

The text of *The Art of Time in Fiction: As Long As It Takes* is set in Warnock Pro, a typeface designed by Robert Slimbach for Adobe Systems in 2000. Book design by Wendy Holdman. Composition by BookMobile Design and Publishing Services, Minneapolis, Minnesota. Manufactured by Versa Press on acid-free paper.